THE QUALITY TIME FAMILY COOKBOOK

JULIE METCALF CULL, R.D.

The Quality Time Family Cookbook: Over 200 Delicious, Healthy, and Fast Famly Favorites for Making Mealtime Creative and Fun
©1995 by Julie Metcalf Cull, R.D.

All rights reserved. Except for brief passages for review purposes, no part of this publication may be reproduced, stored in a retrieval system, or transmitted, in any form or by any means, electronic, photocopying, recording, or otherwise, without the prior written permission of Chronimed Publishing.

Library of Congress Cataloging-in-Publication Data

Julie Metcalf Cull, R.D.
The Quality Time Family Cookbook: Over 200 Delicious, Healthy, and Fast Famly Favorites for Making Mealtime Creative and Fun./Julie Metcalf Cull, R.D.
    p.   cm.
Includes index
ISBN 1-56561-066-0; $12.95

Edited by: Kristin Nelson
Cover Design: Garborg Design Works
Text Design and Production: Janet Hogge
Managing Editor: Donna Hoel
Art/Production Manager: Claire Lewis
Printed in the United States of America

Published by
Chronimed Publishing
P.O. Box 59032
Minneapolis, MN 55459-9686

10 9 8 7 6 5 4 3 2 1

Dedication

This book is dedicated to another era—the one in which I grew up. I can never thank my parents and grandparents enough for giving me such a carefree childhood. I can still feel the summer breezes and hear the wash whipping in the wind. I feel the cool grass under my feet at the end of a day. I hope this book takes you and your family back home with me. If it does, you will have returned to a time when life was less complex and families always enjoyed meals together.

NOTICE:

TAKE SPECIAL PRECAUTIONS WITH CHILDREN UNDER AGE 2. CONSULT A HEALTH CARE PROFESSIONAL.

Many of the recipes in this book are low in fat and may not be appropriate for children less than two years old. Before that age, fat and cholesterol are crucial for healthy cell and brain development. Readers are advised to seek the guidance of a licensed physician or health care professional before making changes in health care regimens. Each individual case or need may vary. This book is intended for informational purposes only and is not for use as an alternative to appropriate medical care. While every effort has been made to ensure that the information is the most current available, new research findings, being released with increased frequency, may invalidate some data.

Acknowledgments

Family, friends, colleagues, patients, and guests at the Parson's Inn in Glen Haven, Wisconsin, provided recipes and encouragement to make *The Quality Time Family Cookbook* a "bible" of family dining themes and great food. I wish I could introduce each of them to you. Their stories have greatly enriched this book.

My mother, Mary Metcalf Huser deserves very special thanks. She carried the load at the Parson's Inn and tested and retested the recipes as I wrote. Thanks, Mom.

Thanks also to Diane Barton, Rose Behrens, Steve Benish, Peggy Biddick, Anne Kriener Blocker, Frannie Blum, Carol Boleyn, Janice Bowers, Connie Burns, Carol Metcalf Cale, Dave, Jackie, Cory, and Chris Cale, Donna Carey, Bernice Cathman, Amy Cherwin, Colleen Chesterman, Mabel Cavianni, John, Annie, and James Cull, Bonnie Cull, Marie Cull, Diana Davis, Debi Edwards, Kathi Edwards, Bernice Ehrlich, Janet Esser, Pat Feldman, Pat Fisher, Barb Flatness, Linda Fontana, Ellen Franklin, Bob and Mary Goodchild, Arletta Giese, Cindy Hatch, Craig, Larry, and Annie Hall, Teresa and Jon Haugen, Diane Hawn, Denny and Alicia Hevey, Rita Holmberg, Peg Howard, Matt and Janie Hundley, Mary Metcalf Huser, Mary Regina Huser, Larry Huser, Kristie Jacobsen, Irma Johnson, Marty and Lisa Kahler, Charlie Keppel, Laurie Kimber, Kay Kingsley, Vivian Klinkhammer, Suzanne Koury, James Lander, Julie Ann Lickteig, Kelly Lutz, Susie Manternach, James Marrari, Virginia and Raymond Mergen, John, Pattie, Andrea, and Aimee Metcalf, Larry and Kristie Metcalf, Sally Metcalf and Sarah, Caroline Mockler, Linda Morgan, Deb Myhre, Pam Myhre, Ramona Pape, David Paul and Kathi McCluskie, Dana Peterson, Susie Poettgen, Linda Root, Karen Ries, Mary Cull Ryan, Barb and Ed Schick, Liane Schmidt, Val Schmidt, Julie Schwendinger, LaVon Scull, Sheri Sheffert, Jane Siebriecht, Kristalyn Sitts, M.J. Smith, Tracy Sukow, Kay Taylor, Mary Teasdale, Karen Klinkhammer Tornowske and Tony, Kathy Udelhofen, Mary Ploessl Vogt, Archie Vorwald, Cheryl Metcalf Wackershauser, Bruce, Eric, and Megan, Jackie Wehrle, Candy Weiland, Becky Welter, Sharon White, and Mary Ann Voels.

Table of Contents

Dedication III

Acknowledgments IV

Foreword VII

Introduction VIII

Changes of Seasons 1
Autumn Tailgate 2
Snowbound, Stranded, and Eskimo Pie 16

Happiness is. 27
Birthday Bash 28
Mother's or Father's Day 37
Romance is in the air 45

Creating Holiday Traditions 53
New Year's Resolutions 54
Ghosts and Goblins 67
Chestnuts Roasting by the Fire 79

Just for Fun 99
Hollywood Favorites 100
Relaxing at the Beach 113
Pizza and Cards 123
Rainy Day Comfort 134

FAVORITE SPORTS … 143

Super Sunday … 144
Bottom of the Ninth Grand Slam … 157
Learning a New Sport … 170

THINGS TO GET DONE … 179

Trash or Treasure … 180
Back to School … 189
County Fair … 199
Holiday Shopping … 209

HEALTHY CHOICES … 221

Home on the Range … 222
Planning the Family Vacation … 231
The Ecology Experience … 238
White House Dining … 250

COMPANY'S COMING … 267

Grandma and Grandpa's Visit … 268
Best Friends Arrive … 280

INDEX … 293

Foreword

Once every so often, an author embarks on a written journey that blends her diverse experiences. As a registered dietitian, Julie Cull is an expert in creating healthy meal plans. As proprietor of the Parson's Inn, a charming bed and breakfast in Glen Haven, Wisconsin, she recognizes that mealtime is a family activity that provides an important opportunity for conversation, fun, and developing a sense of community. Her idea to create a cookbook that advances both nutrition and family therapy is brilliant and unique.

The lack of quality time in families has become a pervasive problem. This straightforward and easy-to-read book offers one solution to this problem. As a guest at the Parson's Inn, I have experienced firsthand the author's ability to blend brilliant meals with warm and pleasant conversation. The spirit of this experience is captured in this book.

A dietitian concerns herself with the nutritional value of a menu, while the proprietor of an inn must concern herself with the presentation, diversity, and flavor of foods. Cull does both as she creates delicious gourmet meals for her guests. *The Quality Time Family Cookbook* presents some of her favorite recipes for you to use as your family learns to enjoy meals together.

The potential benefits of this book for families are numerous and varied. They include:

— Ideas for making family mealtimes a fun and healthy activity. Meals can become entertaining times that stimulate parents and children alike.

— Families with problems, particulary with communicating, will have opportunities to build closeness and reduce the animosity that often takes over family dynamics.

— Both parents and children will learn about healthy eating patterns and associating them with fun.

I want to congratulate Julie Cull for initiating a wonderful idea and seeing it through to a very successful conclusion. Bon apetit!

David S. Paul, Ph.D., Licensed Psychologist
Laurelwood Counseling Center—Westlake, Ohio

INTRODUCTION

Time. There never seems to be enough of it to go around. Whether we're working, running errands, picking up children, making dinner, or trying to save some time for ourselves, it can be difficult to accomplish everything we want (or need) on a daily basis.

Ironically, the less time we have, the more time we seem to need.

The fact is, no matter how busy our days may be, time is most essential with the people we love. It waters the soils of our relationships, can help children grow and mature, and keep our families connected. And it's enjoyable too. The more quality time we share, the better.

A recent *Reader's Digest* poll revealed that children who eat four or more meals each week with their families scored 18% higher in academic tests, compared to those who dine with their families less often.

The Quality Time Family Cookbook is about helping you and your family find creative ways to celebrate time together. It's about planning activities and enjoying nutritious meals, laughing, and living life to its fullest.

Each section is based on a festive theme, then organized by a variety of activities and delectable menu selections. Look through the book to get acquainted with the themes and to find the ones most interesting to you. When you need some suggestions for food and fun, you'll know just where to go! So use the book in the way that works best for you—and have fun!

Changes of Season

Autumn Tailgate
•
Snowbound, Stranded,
& Eskimo Pie

Autumn Tailgate

The reds and golds of autumn have come alive, the smell of grilled food lingers in the air, and everyone is having a ball. It's tailgating time again!

Autumn offers an abundance of opportunities for family food and fun. There are many ways to spend the weekends, but one of our favorites is tailgating with friends and family while our team plays a home game. It's a great way to participate in the crisp outdoors and enjoy favorite fare with people you care about.

The classic tailgate menu includes grilled foods and salads. If you're in the mood for something simple, you may want to include burgers and peppercorn salad. The seasoned tailgater may want to try marinated chicken breasts and homemade potato salad.

Your afternoon menu may also include a warm cup of soup and a peanut butter cookie. Whatever you choose to make, it'll probably be a hit with everyone. Who knows, those great-looking salads and desserts may even attract new acquaintances!

Autumn Tailgate Activities

1. Design a tailgate menu that is agreeable with your taste and your schedule. Choose family favorites that can be made ahead of time or picked up at the deli on the way to the game.

2. Assign grocery shopping and preparation tasks. Break these up to avoid a last minute rush before you leave.

3. Add plenty of ice or ice packs to your grocery list. Put ice cubes in ziplock bags to prevent melting into food. To save money, you can freeze and bag ice for a week ahead. Two-liter plastic soda-pop bottles or milk jugs work well. Generally, foods transported in coolers need to remain below 40° F.

4. Prepare your grill for transport. Be sure to include heat resistant packing material for the trip home. You will also need to anchor the grill so it won't spill.

5. Design banners to cheer your team on to victory.

6. Try to stump your tailgate friends with team trivia.

7. Pack a frisbee or volleyball and a battery-operated radio so you can listen to the pregame broadcast. It's fun to tape the team fight song to replay while you tailgate.

8. Allow plenty of time for the grill to cool down before you go to the game, as well as time to wait in long lines. Go. Fight. Win!

Autumn Tailgate Menus

Pep Rally Supper

* Red Pepper Fish
* Parmesan Potatoes
  Potato Rolls
  Frozen Vanilla Yogurt

Fresh Fruit
Tub Margarine
Skim Milk
Coffee or Tea

Pregame Breakfast

* Apple Cardamom Bread
  Low-Fat Granola Bars
  Frozen Milk Shakes

Beginner's Tailgate Lunch

* Cheesy Potato Soup
  Lean Hamburgers
* Easy Veggie Pizza
* Low-Fat Peanut
  Butter Cookies

Hamburger Buns
Pretzels
Oyster Crackers
Soft Drinks or
Nonalcoholic Beer

"Been at It Longer" Tailgate Lunch

Marinated Chicken Breasts
* Old-Fashioned German
  Potato Salad
* Carol's Peppercorn
  Salad

Hamburger Buns
* Low-Fat Peanut
  Butter Cookies
Soft Drinks or
Nonalcoholic Beer

(* recipe follows)

Pep Rally Supper Recipes

RED PEPPER FISH

1 lb. fresh or frozen cod
1/2 cup water
1/2 cup sherry
1 cup mild salsa or picante sauce
1 red bell pepper, chopped
1/2 medium onion, chopped
1 Tbsp. olive oil
*1 bunch of fresh spinach leaves,
  washed and drained*
Soy sauce

Thaw fish if frozen. Cut into serving size pieces. In a large skillet combine water and sherry. Bring to a low boil. Add fish, then reduce heat. Cover and simmer for 12 to 15 minutes or until fish flakes easily with a fork. Place salsa, chopped pepper and onion, and oil in a small saucepan. Heat through over low heat. Arrange spinach on serving plates. Remove fish from skillet with slotted spatula. Place fish on spinach. Spoon salsa sauce on fillets. Sprinkle with soy sauce. *Preparation time = 10 minutes. Cooking time = 30 minutes.*

NUTRITION FACTS—Serving size = 4 oz. • Servings = 4 • Calories = 224 • Total fat = 5 gm. • Cholesterol = 59 mg. • Sodium = 710 mg. • Total carbohydrate = 11 gm. • Dietary fiber = 2 gm. • Protein = 26 gm.

EXCHANGE VALUES—3 lean meat, 1/2 bread/starch, 1 vegetable

PARMESAN POTATOES

4 medium potatoes
1/4 cup low-fat margarine
1/2 cup chopped onions
3 Tbsp. nonfat Parmesan cheese
2 Tbsp. flour
1/8 tsp. salt
1/4 tsp. pepper

Preheat oven to 350°. Cut potatoes into bite-size chunks. Place in a bowl of water and set aside. Melt margarine in an 8" x 8" baking dish. Layer onions in bottom of baking dish. Mix cheese, flour, salt, and pepper together. Drain potato pieces on a paper towel. Shake potatoes and cheese mixture in a plastic bag. Place coated potato pieces on top of onions. Sprinkle any remaining cheese mixture over potatoes. Bake for 45 minutes, stirring every 15 minutes. *Preparation time = 15 minutes. Baking time = 45 minutes.*

NUTRITION FACTS—Serving Size = 1/2 cup • Servings = 8 • Calories = 113 • Total fat = 3 gm. • Cholesterol = 2 mg. • Sodium = 102 mg. • Total carbohydrate = 20 gm. • Dietary fiber = 1.5 gm. • Protein = 2.5 gm.

EXCHANGE VALUES—1 bread/starch, 1/2 fat

Pregame Breakfast Recipes

APPLE CARDAMOM BREAD

2 cups flour
1 tsp. baking soda
1/2 tsp. salt
1/2 tsp. baking powder
1 tsp. cinnamon
1 tsp. cardamom
1/4 cup low-fat margarine
1/4 cup plain yogurt
3/4 cup brown sugar
1 tsp. orange rind, grated
1/4 cup orange juice
2 eggs (or 1/2 cup liquid egg substitute)
1 tsp. vanilla
2 cups chopped apples
1/3 cup chopped walnuts
Nonstick cooking spray

Preheat oven to 350°. Mix dry ingredients together, then set aside. Mix margarine, yogurt, brown sugar, orange rind, orange juice, eggs, and vanilla together. Add dry ingredients to mixture. Fold in chopped apples and walnuts. Place mixture in two small loaf pans (8 1/2" x 4 1/2" x 2 1/2") coated with nonstick cooking spray. Bake 40 to 45 minutes. *Preparation time = 15 minutes. Baking time = 45 minutes.*

NUTRITION FACTS—Serving size = 1/10 of loaf • Servings = 20 • Calories = 133 • Total fat = 4 gm. • Cholesterol (with egg) = 22 mg. • Cholesterol (with egg substitute) = <1 mg. • Sodium = 160 mg. • Total carbohydrate = 22 gm. • Dietary fiber = 1 gm • Protein = 3 gm.

EXCHANGE VALUES—1 bread/starch, 1/2 fruit, 1/2 fat

Beginner's Tailgate Lunch Recipes

CHEESY POTATO SOUP

6 medium potatoes, cubed
1 cup onion, chopped
1 cup celery, diced
1 medium carrot, sliced
3/4 tsp. salt
2 cups water
2 cups skim milk
3 Tbsp. low-fat margarine
1/8 tsp. white pepper
1/2 cup nonfat grated pizza cheese

Combine potatoes, onion, celery, carrot, salt, and water. Cook 20 minutes or until tender. Add skim milk, margarine, and pepper; reheat. Sprinkle each serving with 1 1/2 tablespoons grated cheese. Flavor is better if made the day before. *Preparation time = 15 minutes. Cooking time = 25 minutes.*

NUTRITION FACTS—Serving size = 1/2 cup • Servings = 12 • Calories = 103 • Total fat = 1.5 gm. • Cholesterol = 1.5 mg. • Sodium = 235 mg. • Total carbohydrate = 18 gm. • Dietary fiber = 1.5 gm. • Protein = 4.5 gm.

EXCHANGE VALUES—1 bread/starch, 1/2 lean meat

EASY VEGGIE PIZZA

12-inch whole wheat pizza crust, prebaked
3/4 cup low-fat mayonnaise
1 cup nonfat sour cream
1 Tbsp. dill weed
1 tsp. garlic powder
1 Tbsp. onion powder
1 1/2 cup cauliflower
1 1/2 cup broccoli
1 1/2 cup carrots or celery, chopped
8 to 10 cherry tomatoes, halved (or 1 medium tomato, thinly cut)
1 cup nonfat mild cheddar cheese, shredded

Combine mayonnaise, sour cream, and spices, and spread on whole wheat pizza crust (recipe on next page). Arrange vegetables on sour cream mixture. Sprinkle with cheese. Refrigerate until serving time. *Preparation time = 20 minutes.*

NUTRITION FACTS—(Nutrition facts are for pizza topping alone. Nutrition facts for pizza are on next page.)—Serving size = 1/12 of pizza • Servings = 12 • Calories = 48 • Total fat = <1 gm. • Cholesterol = 0 mg. • Sodium = 119 mg. • Total carbohydrate = 8 gm. • Dietary fiber = 2 gm. • Protein = 5 gm.

EXCHANGE VALUES—2 vegetable (without crust)

WHOLE WHEAT PIZZA CRUST

>1 package quick-acting dry yeast
>1 cup warm water
>2 tsp. sugar
>1 tsp. salt
>1 Tbsp. oil
>1 cup white flour
>2 cups whole wheat flour

Preheat oven to 450°. Combine water, sugar, and yeast in a large bowl. (Make sure water is not too hot or it will kill the yeast.) When yeast is dissolved, add salt, oil, and one cup white flour. Mix until smooth, then add whole wheat flour. Knead until elastic (about five minutes). Place in a greased bowl; grease top of dough, and let rise until double its original size, about 45 minutes (it will rise faster if you set it in a warm place). Form into two balls. Pat and stretch onto two 12" pizza pans. Let rest 10 minutes before baking. Bake for 10 to 12 minutes or until crust starts to brown. Cool. Prepare with your favorite toppings or freeze for future use. *Preparation time = 15 minutes. Rising time = 1 hour. Baking time = 12 minutes.*

NUTRITION FACTS—Serving size = 3-inch wedge • Servings = 12 • Calories = 64 • Total fat = <1 gm. • Cholesterol = 0 mg. • Sodium = 89 mg. • Total carbohydrate = 13 gm. • Dietary fiber = <1 gm. • Protein = 2 gm.

EXCHANGE VALUES—1 bread/starch without veggie mixture; 1 bread/starch, 2 vegetables with veggies

LOW-FAT PEANUT BUTTER COOKIES

1/2 cup low-fat vanilla yogurt
1/2 cup low-fat peanut butter, smooth or chunky
1 cup brown sugar, firmly packed
1 egg (or 1/4 cup liquid egg substitute)
1 1/2 cup flour
1/2 tsp. baking powder
3/4 tsp. baking soda
1/4 tsp. salt
Nonstick cooking spray

Preheat oven to 350°. Mix yogurt, peanut butter, brown sugar, and egg together. Stir in dry ingredients. Chill dough for 3 hours or overnight. Drop dough by rounded tablespoonfuls onto a baking sheet that has been sprayed with nonstick cooking spray. Bake for 10 to 12 minutes or until golden brown. Place on to a wire rack and cool. *Preparation time = 10 minutes. Baking time = 12 minutes.*

NUTRITION FACTS—Serving size = 1 cookie • Servings = 36 • Calories = 70 • Total fat = 2 gm. • Cholesterol (with egg) = 6 gm. • Cholesterol (with egg substitute) = < 1 gm. • Sodium = 68 mg. • Total carbohydrate = 11 gm. • Dietary fiber = < 1 gm. • Protein = 2 gm.

EXCHANGE VALUES—1 bread/starch

"Been at It Longer" Tailgate Lunch Recipes

OLD-FASHIONED GERMAN POTATO SALAD

6 medium potatoes
3 slices bacon
1/2 cup cider vinegar
1/4 cup sugar
1/2 cup onion, chopped
1/2 tsp. salt
1 1/2 heaping Tbsp. flour
1/8 tsp. pepper (optional)

Boil potatoes in their skins; drain and let cool. Brown bacon until crisp; cool, then break into small pieces. Combine vinegar, sugar, onion, salt, and bacon. Heat mixture and stir in flour until slightly thickened. Cube or slice potatoes and pour warm vinegar mixture over potatoes. Shake a small amount of pepper over salad, if desired. Serve hot.

If made ahead, this salad can be microwaved for several minutes until heated thoroughly. *Preparation time = 30 minutes.*

NUTRITION FACTS—Serving size = 1/2 cup • Servings = 8 • Calories = 134 • Total fat = 1 gm. • Cholesterol = 2 mg. • Sodium = 176 mg. • Total carbohydrate = 29 gm. • Dietary fiber = 2 gm. • Protein = 3 gm.

EXCHANGE VALUES—1 1/2 bread/starch

CAROL'S PEPPERCORN SALAD

2 cups colored rotini pasta
2 cups red cabbage, chopped coarsely
2 cups green cabbage, chopped coarsely
4 cups fresh spinach, torn into 1 1/2" pieces
7 green onions, chopped into 1/2" pieces
15 to 20 cherry tomatoes
1 1/2 cups low-fat cheddar cheese, cubed
1 to 1 1/2 cups fat-free or nonfat peppercorn dressing

Cook rotini about 10 minutes, drain and cool. Set aside. Toss remaining ingredients together. Refrigerate for at least an hour. Taste and add more peppercorn dressing as desired. Keeps for several days. *Preparation time = 20 minutes. Refrigeration time = 1 hour.*

NUTRITION FACTS—Serving size = 1 cup • Servings = 16 • Calories = 162 • Total fat = 4 gm. • Cholesterol = 15 mg. • Sodium = 493 mg. • Total carbohydrate = 22 gm. • Dietary fiber = 5 gm. • Protein = 11 gm.

EXCHANGE VALUES—1 bread/starch, 2 vegetable, 1 fat

Autumn Tailgate Shopping List

Take this book with you to your supermarket or photocopy the list. Select the same number or size of items you have in the past, based on the number of people you are shopping for. Review this list before you go to the store. Cross out items you have on hand, and write in your personal likes and needs.

Produce

Onions
Carrots
Cherry tomatoes
Red cabbage
Green cabbage
Broccoli
Celery
Green onions
Bunch fresh spinach leaves
Apples
Cauliflower
Red bell pepper
Fresh fruit
Potatoes

Packaged

Walnuts
Colored rotini pasta
Granola bars
Oyster crackers
Nonfat Parmesan cheese

Staples/Spices

Black pepper
White pepper
Salt
Soy sauce
Basil
Whole wheat flour
All purpose flour
Baking soda
Baking powder
Quick-acting dry yeast
Cinnamon
Cardamom
Dill weed
Garlic powder
Onion powder
Grated orange rind
Vanilla
Olive oil
Granulated sugar
Brown sugar
Oil
Nonstick cooking spray
Cider vinegar

Bottled/Canned

Low-fat peanut butter, smooth
  or chunky
Fat-free peppercorn dressing
Mild salsa or picante
Low-fat mayonnaise

Frozen Case

Orange juice
Vanilla ice milk
Frozen milk shakes

Refrigerator Case

Low-fat margarine
Nonfat cream cheese
Shredded low-fat
  cheddar cheese
Plain yogurt
Eggs or egg substitute
Skim milk
Grated nonfat pizza cheese
Low-fat vanilla yogurt
Nonfat sour cream
Low-fat cheddar cheese

Meat Case

Fresh or frozen cod
Bacon
Lean ground beef

Bakery/Deli

Potato rolls
Hamburger buns
Marinated chicken breasts

Snack Foods

Pretzels

Other

Sherry
Nonalcoholic beer
Soft drinks

Snowbound, Stranded, and Eskimo Pie

The ground is knee-deep in snow, the air is chilly, and the last thing anyone wants to do is travel (beyond the backyard, of course). 'Tis the season—enjoy it while you can!

Winter is a time to bundle up and stay warm; it's also a time to enjoy the outdoors. If you decide to venture out for a tobogganing run or just to play outside, chances are you'll have a hearty appetite when you return to the warmth of your home.

Planning meals during this homebound period may mean relying on a well-stocked pantry, refrigerator, and freezer. The menus in this section are created to be simple, so you can spend the rest of your day playing board games and watching old movies.

Top any of these meals with an ice cream treat. After a day of playing in the snow, nothing could taste better than hot chocolate and an Eskimo Pie!

Snowbound, Stranded, and Eskimo Pie Activities

1. Build a fort with your children. Design windows, doors, and a roof. If you decide to use the fort, put blankets on the floor inside. Bring in lawn furniture or sit on blankets on the snow floor.

2. Build a snow family resembling your own. Trim each snow person with old clothing items and props that match the interests and hobbies of your family members.

3. Play fox and goose in the snow. Stomp out a large circle, then make intersecting foot tracks to the middle of the circle. Choose one person to be "it." He or she tags another using only these paths.

4. Make snow angels. Lay flat on your back and spread your arms up and down like wings. Put food coloring in a spray bottle filled with water and spray your angel impression.

5. Offer to shovel your neighbor's sidewalk.

Snowbound, Stranded, and Eskimo Pie Menu

Winter Winds Dinner

* Kay's Shrimp and Angel Hair
  Cream-Style Corn
* Pea and Cheese Salad
  Bread Sticks
* Low-Fat Chocolate Chip Cookies
  Skim Milk
  Coffee or Tea

Snow Drift Breakfast

* Western Omelettes
* Cheesecake Pie
  Fresh Fruit Platter

  Coffee or Tea
  Grape Juice

Board Game Sunday

* Tangy Chicken Breasts
  Baked Potatoes
  Nonfat Sour Cream
  Low-Fat Hot Chocolate and Marshmallows

  Lettuce Salad
  Nonfat Ranch Dressing
* Raisin Oatmeal Muffins
  Eskimo Pies

(* recipe follows)

Changes of Season

Winter Winds Dinner Recipes

KAY'S SHRIMP AND ANGEL HAIR

1/2 lb. angel hair spaghetti, (dry or fresh)
2 Tbsp. olive oil
4 large cloves garlic, chopped (or 2 tsp. instant garlic)
20 medium shrimp, peeled and deveined
1/4 tsp. salt
1/2 tsp. pepper
1 tsp. curry powder
2 Tbsp. fresh cilantro
1/4 cup Parmesan cheese, grated

In large saucepan, bring 3 quarts water to a boil. Add spaghetti and cook until tender but still firm (8 to 10 minutes). Meanwhile, heat olive oil over medium heat in a large skillet. Add garlic and cook until softened and slightly browned. Add shrimp, salt, pepper, curry powder, and cilantro. Cook mixture 1 to 3 minutes until shrimp turn pink. Remove skillet from heat.

Drain spaghetti and put in a large bowl; pour shrimp mixture over noodles and toss. Sprinkle with Parmesan cheese. *Preparation time = 20 minutes.*

NUTRITION FACTS—Serving size = 1 1/2 cups • Servings = 4 • Calories = 300 • Total fat = 10 gm. • Saturated fat = 8 gm. • Cholesterol = 47 mg. • Sodium = 480 mg. • Total carbohydrate = 37 gm. • Dietary fiber = 1 gm. • Protein = 13 gm.

EXCHANGE VALUES—2 bread/starch, 1 lean meat, 2 fat

PEA AND CHEESE SALAD

*9-oz. package frozen green peas
   (or 1 1/2 cups fresh peas)
1 cup low-fat farmer's cheese,
   cubed (approx. 5 oz.)
1/2 cup sweet onion, chopped
1/2 cup sweet yellow pepper, chopped
1/3 cup nonfat ranch dressing*

Mix all ingredients several hours before serving for best taste. Refrigerate. *Preparation time = 10 minutes.*

NUTRITION FACTS—Serving size = 1/2 cup • Servings = 5 • Calories = 170 • Total fat = 3 gm. • Cholesterol = 15 mg. • Sodium = 400 mg. • Total carbohydrate = 12 gm. • Dietary fiber = <1 gm. • Protein = 23 gm.

EXCHANGE VALUES—1/2 bread/starch, 2 1/2 lean meat, 1/2 fat

LOW-FAT CHOCOLATE CHIP COOKIES

1/2 cup low-fat margarine
3/4 cup brown sugar
1 egg (or 1/4 cup egg substitute)
1 tsp. vanilla
1 1/2 cup flour
1/2 tsp. soda
1/2 tsp. salt
3/4 cup mini chocolate chips
Nonstick cooking spray

Preheat oven to 350°. Spray cookie sheets with nonstick cooking spray. Combine margarine, brown sugar, egg, and vanilla. Add dry ingredients and mix well. Fold in chocolate chips. Bake 8 to 10 minutes or until golden brown. Note: If you use a nonstick cookie sheet, you don't need nonstick cooking spray. *Preparation time = 10 minutes. Baking time = 10 minutes.*

NUTRITION FACTS—Serving size = 1 cookie • Servings = 36 • Calories = 76 • Total fat = 4 gm. • Cholesterol (with egg) = 6 mg. • Cholesterol (with egg substitute) = 0 mg. • Sodium = 73 mg. • Total carbohydrate = 11 gm. • Dietary fiber = <1 gm. • Protein = <1 gm.

EXCHANGE VALUES—1 bread/starch, 1/2 fat

Snow Drift Breakfast Recipes

WESTERN OMELETTE

1 large tomato, chopped
1/2 medium green pepper, chopped
1 4-oz. can sliced mushrooms, drained
6 eggs (or 1 1/2 cups liquid egg substitute)
1 Tbsp. water
1/4 tsp. salt
1/4 cup medium salsa
Nonstick cooking spray

Combine tomato, green pepper, and mushrooms; set aside. In another bowl, combine eggs, water, and salt. Using a fork, beat until mixed but not frothy. Combine vegetables with egg mixture. Heat nonstick skillet to medium heat; add egg mixture. Tilt pan to coat sides. Run a spatula around the edge of the skillet. When eggs are set but still shiny, spoon vegetable filling across center of omelette. Fold omelette in half. Transfer onto a warm platter. Top with salsa. *Preparation time = 15 minutes.*

NUTRITION FACTS—Serving size = 1/4 omelette • Servings = 4 • Calories = 111 • Total fat = 3 gm. • Cholesterol (with egg) = 366 mg. • Cholesterol (with egg substitute) = 1 mg. • Sodium = 451 mg. • Total carbohydrate = 8 gm. • Dietary fiber = 1 gm. • Protein = 13 gm.

EXCHANGE VALUES—2 lean meat

CHEESECAKE PIE

8-inch graham cracker pie crust
3/4 tsp. cinnamon
1/2 cup raisins
1 1/2 cups low-fat ricotta cheese
2 Tbsp. rum
1 Tbsp. orange rind, grated
1 Tbsp. orange juice, squeezed
1 Tbsp. honey
1/2 tsp. cinnamon
1/4 tsp. ginger
1/3 cup soda cracker crumbs
1/4 tsp. pine nuts

Preheat oven to 350°. Sprinkle 3/4 tsp. cinnamon in bottom of pie crust. Microwave raisins in 1/2 cup water for 2 minutes on high; drain. Combine raisins with all remaining ingredients except pine nuts. Put into pie crust and sprinkle with pine nuts. Bake for 30 to 35 minutes. Pie should be golden brown. *Preparation time = 15 minutes. Baking time = 35 minutes.*

NUTRITION FACTS—Serving size = 1/8 of pie • Servings = 8 • Calories = 215 • Total fat = 8.8 gm. • Cholesterol = 14 mg. • Sodium = 169 mg. • Total carbohydrate = 27 gm. • Dietary fiber = 2 gm. • Protein = 7 gm.

EXCHANGE VALUES—2 bread/starch, 1 1/2 fat

Sunday Board Game Recipes

TANGY CHICKEN BREASTS

3/4 cup unseasoned dry bread crumbs
1 tsp. cinnamon
1 tsp. nutmeg
1 tsp. garlic powder
1/2 tsp. ginger
1/2 tsp. salt
1 egg (or 1/4 cup liquid egg substitute)
2/3 cup orange juice
1/3 cup low-fat margarine
8 skinless chicken breasts (about 3 to 4 oz. each)
Nonstick cooking spray

Preheat oven to 350°. Place bread crumbs in a mixing bowl. Add spices and salt. Mix well. Set aside. Beat egg, then add orange juice. Dip each chicken breast in egg and orange juice mixture. Coat with spicy bread crumb mixture. Melt margarine in a nonstick skillet. Add chicken breasts and brown on both sides. Place in a 9" x 13" pan sprayed with nonstick cooking spray. Bake for 1/2 hour covered, then uncover and bake for another 1/2 hour. *Preparation time = 20 minutes. Baking time = 1 hour.*

NUTRITION FACTS—Serving size = 1 piece • Servings = 8 • Calories = 321 • Total fat = 10 gm. • Cholesterol (with egg) = 123 mg. • Cholesterol (with egg substitute) = 92 mg. • Sodium = 468 mg. • Total carbohydrate = 18 gm. • Dietary fiber <1 gm. • Protein = 39 gm.

EXCHANGE VALUES—4 lean meat, 1 bread/starch, 1/2 fat

RAISIN OATMEAL MUFFINS

1/2 cup raisins
1 cup water
1 medium apple, peeled and chopped
1/3 cup brown sugar
1/2 cup skim milk
2 eggs (or 1/2 cup liquid egg substitute)
2 Tbsp. low-fat margarine
3/4 cup flour
1/2 tsp. baking powder
1/4 tsp. salt
1 tsp. baking soda
1 tsp. cinnamon
3/4 cup oatmeal
Nonstick cooking spray

Preheat oven to 350°. Prepare 12 muffin cups with paper liners or by spraying with nonstick cooking spray. Microwave raisins in one cup of water for 2 to 3 minutes on high; drain, and set aside. Peel and chop apple. Set aside. In mixing bowl, combine brown sugar, milk, eggs, margarine, and apple. Set aside. Combine dry ingredients. Add raisins to egg and milk mixture. Gently fold in dry ingredients; avoid overbeating. Spoon about 2/3 cup into each muffin cup. Bake for about 20 minutes or until muffins are golden. *Preparation time = 15 minutes. Baking time = 20 minutes.*

NUTRITION FACTS—Serving size = 1 muffin • Servings = 12 • Calories = 121 • Total fat = 3 gm. • Cholesterol (with egg) = 36 mg. • Cholesterol (with egg substitute) = 0 • Sodium = 207 mg. • Total carbohydrate = 21 gm. • Dietary fiber = <1 gm. • Protein = 3 gm.

EXCHANGE VALUES—1 bread/starch, 1/2 fruit, 1/2 fat

Snowbound, Stranded, and Eskimo Pie Shopping List

Take this book along to your supermarket or photocopy the list. Select the same number or size of items that you have in the past, based on the number of people you are shopping for. Review this list before you go to the store. Cross out items you have on hand, and write in your personal likes and needs.

Produce

Cilantro
Garlic
Apple
Orange
Sweet onion
Sweet yellow pepper
Green pepper
Tomato
Lettuce
Potatoes
Fresh fruit

Packaged

Angel hair spaghetti
Mini chocolate chips
Graham cracker crust
Soda cracker crumbs
Low-fat hot chocolate
  drink mix
Pine nuts
Unseasoned bread crumbs
Raisins
Oatmeal
Coffee
Tea
Marshmallows

Staples/Spices

Salt
Pepper
Brown sugar
Vanilla
Flour
Baking soda
Baking powder
Cinnamon
Ginger
Nutmeg
Garlic powder
Grated orange rind
Olive oil
Curry powder
Nonstick cooking spray

Bottled/Canned

Cream-style corn
Nonfat ranch dressing
Canned mushrooms
Salsa, medium

Frozen Case

Frozen peas
Orange juice
Eskimo Pies

Refrigerator Case

Low-fat margarine
Low-fat ricotta cheese
Low-fat farmer's cheese
Skim milk
Grape juice
Nonfat sour cream
Eggs or egg substitute
Parmesan cheese, grated

Meat Case

Medium shrimp
Skinless chicken breasts

Bakery/Deli

Bread sticks

Other

Rum

Happiness Is...

- BIRTHDAY BASH
- MOTHER'S OR FATHER'S DAY
- ROMANCE IS IN THE AIR

BIRTHDAY BASH

The candles are lit, banners are up, confetti is covering the table, and laughter permeates the air. Family and friends watch as the birthday guest blows out the candles and makes a wish. It's another great birthday party!

Everyone loves a birthday. For young people, especially, it's an exciting day of smiles, gifts, cake, and lots of special people. But whether young or old, people delight in this tribute to "their day." Our family loves it because we can show the honored guest how much they mean to us by really celebrating them!

The recipes in this section are some of our birthday favorites. We hope you enjoy them as much as we have.

BIRTHDAY BASH ACTIVITIES

1. Before planning a birthday celebration, determine whether the birthday guest would enjoy a celebration with a small group or a larger one.

2. Delegate some of the responsibilities to others; one person can be in charge of gathering ideas for games, and another can plan the goodies that will be served throughout the day.

3. If it's your child's year to have a "friends-from-school" birthday party, be sure to schedule a family get-together too, no matter how small.

4. You may want to discuss a family budget regarding the celebration. Remember, decorations can be as simple as paper-punch confetti spread on tables and the floor. Have fun while you're decorating.

5. Listen throughout the year to what each family member says about things he or she needs, or trips that person would like to

take. Keep lists of potential gifts and little quotes that can be shared later.

6. Older family members may enjoy a birthday roast. Do a "this is your life in pictures." Suggest having family members and friends describe special memories they have shared with the birthday person.
7. Teach your young children to receive gifts graciously. The gift-giver should always receive a verbal thank you.

Birthday Bash Menu

Excitement-Builds Lunch

* Italian Pasta With Chicken
  Potato Roll
* Cinnamon-Basil Nectarine Pie

Green Beans
Skim Milk
Coffee or Tea

Birthday Party Celebration

Specially Decorated Birthday Cake
Low-Fat Frozen Yogurt
* Banana-Kiwi Malts

One Year Older Sleep-In

* Cilantro Eggs
* Fruity Coffee Cake
  Orange Juice
  Skim Milk
  Coffee or Tea

(* recipe follows)

Excitement Builds Recipes

ITALIAN PASTA WITH CHICKEN

>2 Tbsp. low-fat margarine
>1 lb. boneless chicken breasts, chopped
>1 Tbsp. lemon basil, chopped
>1/2 cup onion, chopped
>1 tsp. garlic, chopped
>3 cups (30 oz. jar) spaghetti sauce
>8-oz. package thin spaghetti
>1 Tbsp. Parmesan cheese, grated

In large skillet, melt margarine. Add chicken, lemon basil, onion, and garlic; cook until chicken is tender. Stir in spaghetti sauce. Reduce heat and cover; simmer, stirring frequently for 10 minutes. Meanwhile, cook pasta according to package directions; drain. Serve sauce over hot pasta; sprinkle with Parmesan cheese. *Preparation time = 15 minutes. Cooking time = 15 minutes.*

NUTRITION FACTS
Serving size = 2 cups • Servings = 5 • Calories = 253 • Total fat = 8 gm. • Cholesterol = 45 mg. • Sodium = 582 mg. • Total carbohydrate = 26 gm. • Dietary fiber = <1 gm. • Protein = 20 gm.

EXCHANGE VALUES—1 1/2 bread/starch, 2 lean meat, 1 fat

CINNAMON-BASIL NECTARINE PIE

8-inch graham cracker crust
1 cup fresh nectarines, finely chopped (2 large)
1/2 cup water
1 cup low-fat cottage cheese
1 cup low-fat vanilla yogurt
2 Tbsp. fresh cinnamon basil, chopped
1/4 cup sugar
1 tsp. vanilla
1/4 cup cold water
1 envelope unflavored gelatin
Dash of nutmeg
12 slices nectarine (for garnish)
5 medium sprigs fresh cinnamon basil (for garnish)

Finely chop nectarines in blender with 1/2 cup water; then drain thoroughly. Thoroughly blend cottage cheese, yogurt, cinnamon basil, sugar, and vanilla in food processor. Place 1/4 cup cold water and gelatin in a small pan over medium heat. Stir gelatin mixture for several minutes until blended, then add to cottage cheese mixture; mix well. Spread drained nectarines in bottom of pie crust, then pour cottage mixture over nectarines. Sprinkle with nutmeg. Cover and refrigerate for at least an hour or overnight. Garnish with additional nectarines and cinnamon basil sprigs. May be made night before. *Preparation time = 15 minutes. Refrigeration time = 1 hour.*

NUTRITION FACTS—Serving size = 1/8 pie • Servings = 8 • Calories = 210 • Total fat = 6 gm. • Cholesterol = 3 mg. • Sodium = 250 mg. • Total carbohydrate = 29 gm. • Dietary fiber = 2 gm. • Protein = 9 gm.

EXCHANGE VALUES—2 bread/starch, 1 fat

Birthday Party Celebration Recipes

BANANA-KIWI MALT

>2 kiwi, peeled and sliced
>1 ripe banana, peeled
>1/2 cup plain low-fat yogurt
>3 ice cubes
>4 large strawberries (for garnish)

Combine first 4 ingredients in blender; puree until smooth. Pour into glasses. Garnish with strawberries. *Preparation time = 10 minutes.*

NUTRITION FACTS—Serving size = 1 cup • Servings = 2 • Calories = 140 • Total fat = 2 gm. • Cholesterol = 4 mg. • Sodium = 44 mg. • Total carbohydrate = 30 gm. • Dietary fiber = 4 gm. • Protein = 4 gm.

EXCHANGE VALUES—1 1/2 fruit, 1/2 skim milk

One Year Older Sleep-In Recipes

CILANTRO EGGS

4 eggs (or 1 cup liquid egg substitute)
2 Tbsp. skim milk
1 tsp. garlic powder
1 tsp. onion powder
1/4 tsp. salt
1/3 cup cilantro, packed fully
2 tsp. olive oil

Beat eggs, then add other ingredients. Heat olive oil in a nonstick pan. Add egg mixture; cook over medium heat. Use a rubber spatula and stir until eggs are firm. *Preparation time = 10 minutes. Cooking time = 5 minutes.*

NUTRITION FACTS—Serving size = 1/2 cup • Servings = 4 • Calories = 116 • Total fat = 7 gm. • Cholesterol (with egg) = 213 mg. • Cholesterol (with egg substitute) = 170 mg. • Sodium = 206 mg. • Total carbohydrate = 2 gm. • Dietary fiber = 0 • Protein = 7 gm.

EXCHANGE VALUES—1 medium fat meat, 2 fat

HAPPINESS IS. . .

FRUITY COFFEE CAKE

>1/2 cup low-fat margarine
>1/2 cup low-fat sour cream
>1/4 cup brown sugar
>2 eggs (or 1/2 cup liquid egg substitute)
>2 cups flour
>1 tsp. baking soda
>1/2 tsp. salt
>1 tsp. nutmeg
>16-oz. can fruit cocktail (in own syrup or water-packed)
>Nonstick cooking spray

Preheat oven to 350°. Cream margarine, sour cream, brown sugar, and eggs together. Add dry ingredients, then fold fruit in last. Spray a 9" x 13" pan with nonstick cooking spray. Add batter and bake uncovered for 30 minutes. Let cool. Cover leftovers after serving. *Preparation time = 10 minutes. Baking time = 30 minutes.*

NUTRITION FACTS—Serving size = 1 slice • Servings = 20 • Calories = 101 • Total fat = 3 gm. • Cholesterol (with egg) = 21 mg. • Cholesterol (with egg substitute) = 0 mg. • Sodium = 168 mg. • Total carbohydrate = <1 gm. • Dietary fiber = <1 gm. • Protein = 2 gm.

EXCHANGE VALUES—1 bread/starch, 1/2 fat

BIRTHDAY BASH SHOPPING LIST

Take this book along to your supermarket or photocopy the list. Select the same number or size of items that you have in the past, based on the number of people for whom you are shopping. Review this list before you go to the store. Cross out items you have on hand, and write in your personal likes and needs.

PRODUCE

Cilantro
Onion
Large nectarines
Kiwi
Bananas
Strawberries
Garlic

PACKAGED

Thin spaghetti
Graham cracker crust
Unflavored gelatin
Coffee
Tea

STAPLES/SPICES

Lemon basil
Fresh cinnamon basil
Garlic powder
Onion powder
Salt
Nutmeg

Baking soda
Brown sugar
Flour
Olive oil
Sugar
Vanilla
Nonstick cooking spay

BOTTLED/CANNED

Spaghetti sauce
Fruit cocktail

FROZEN CASE

Green beans
Low-fat frozen yogurt
Orange juice

HAPPINESS IS. . .

Refrigerator Case

Low-fat cottage cheese
Low-fat vanilla yogurt
Low-fat plain yogurt
Eggs or egg substitute
Skim milk
Low-fat sour cream
Low-fat margarine
Parmesan cheese, grated

Meat Case

Boneless chicken breasts

Bakery/Deli

Potato rolls
Birthday cake

Mother's or Father's Day

The morning has come; a heavenly scent creates a presence throughout the house and a tray of luscious cuisine is about to be served. What a wonderful day to honor a special parent.

Breakfast in bed is always a treat, especially on Mother's or Father's Day. It's a time when children can enjoy planning a special morning for their parent (or guardian), and when parents love to be surprised.

Depending on the age of your children, they may need some guidance from an older child or parent, but if the child has a good idea and can keep a secret, the surprise will most surely be a great one (and parents usually recognize good intentions).

Mother's or Father's Day Activities For Older Children:

1. Decide on the meal you will prepare for the special parent or guardian. You may need another adult to guide you in food preparation.

2. Plan a simple menu. Include the person's favorite foods. If a recipe is complicated for you to prepare, consider special ordering it at the local deli.

3. Tell a parent or adult about your intentions, so everyone is comfortable with the plan. If you're planning a surprise, just indicate when you would like the honoree to be at home.

4. Review the menu and list all food preparation tasks. It's helpful to decide at what time you need to start each task. Start with the recipe that takes the longest to prepare. Work toward the

time you plan to serve. Don't forget to schedule setting the breakfast tray or table.

5. Let your creative thoughts flow. Make the meal or snack attractive. The way you present your meal will be as much of a surprise as what you decide to fix. Remember, people eat first with their noses, then with their eyes, and finally with their mouths.
6. Make a card with your thoughtful words written inside.
7. Gift ideas include corsages or a flower bouquet for women and plants for men.

Mother's or Father's Day Menu

Surprise Breakfast in Bed

Belgian Waffles
Low-Calorie Whipped Topping

* Sugared Blueberries
Orange Juice

Kids Make Lunch

* Mexicali Chicken
Oven-Baked Bread Sticks
Skim Milk

Sliced Kiwi
Vanilla Pudding

After-Church Brunch

* Strawberry Soup
* Shrimpy Cucumber Mint Sandwiches
Hot Apple Cider

(* recipe follows)

Surprise Breakfast in Bed Recipes

SUGARED BLUEBERRIES

16-oz. package frozen blueberries (no sugar)
1 Tbsp. lemon juice
1/2 cup sugar
3 Tbsp. cornstarch

Combine all ingredients and cook over medium heat, stirring frequently until thickened. *Preparation time = 5 minutes. Cooking time = 7 minutes.*

NUTRITION FACTS—Serving size = 1/2 cup • Servings = 4 • Calories = 180 • Total fat = <1 gm. • Cholesterol = 0 mg. • Sodium = 2 mg. • Total carbohydrate =45 gm. • Dietary fiber = <1 gm. • Protein = <1 gm.

EXCHANGE VALUES—2 1/2 bread/starch

NOTE: THIS RECIPE MAY NOT BE SUITABLE FOR INDIVIDUALS WITH ELEVATED BLOOD SUGAR OR TRIGLYCERIDES.

HAPPINESS IS. . .

Kids Make Lunch Recipes

MEXICALI CHICKEN

2 Tbsp. olive oil
3 lbs. boneless, skinless chicken breast
1/4 cup water
1 large onion, chopped
1 large green pepper, cut in julienne strips
1 large sweet yellow pepper, cut in julienne strips
3 tsp. chili powder
1/4 cup flour
8-oz. can low-salt tomatoes
1/4 tsp. salt
1 tsp. sugar
1/4 tsp. pepper
Nonstick cooking spray

Heat olive oil in a heavy fry pan. Brown chicken in oil, then remove chicken and layer it in a cake pan or baking dish sprayed with nonstick cooking spray. Add 1/4 cup water to drippings and sauté the onion and peppers. Stir in chili powder. Add flour and water first, then tomatoes, salt, sugar, and black pepper. Cook, stirring constantly, until sauce thickens. Remove from heat. Pour sauce over chicken and cover. Bake 1 hour at 350°. Uncover and bake 30 minutes longer or until chicken is tender and sauce is thickened slightly. Garnish with red and green pepper rings. *Preparation time = 30 minutes. Baking time = 1 1/2 hours.*

NUTRITION FACTS—Serving size = 3 oz. chicken plus 1/4 cup sauce • Servings = 12 • Calories = 245 • Total fat = 7 gm. • Cholesterol = 96 mg. • Sodium = 139 mg. • Total carbohydrate = 9 gm. • Dietary fiber = 2 gm. • Protein = 36 gm.

EXCHANGE VALUES—3 1/2 lean meat, 1 fat

After-Church Brunch Recipes

STRAWBERRY SOUP

2 10-oz. packages frozen strawberries, thawed
2 cups water
1/4 cup sugar
2 Tbsp. quick-cooking tapioca
Dash of salt
1 Tbsp. lemon juice
1 tsp. cinnamon
11-oz. can mandarin orange sections (about 1 cup)
1 cup canned grapefruit sections
1 kiwi, peeled and cut
1/2 cup fresh strawberries

Blend strawberries until smooth, then pour into a saucepan. Add water, sugar, tapioca, and salt; let stand 5 minutes. Bring to a boil over medium heat, stirring constantly. Remove from heat and add lemon juice and cinnamon. Chill sauce. Add orange and grapefruit sections, kiwi, and fresh strawberries just before serving. *Preparation time = 15 minutes. Chilling time = 30 minutes.*

NUTRITION FACTS—Serving size = 1 cup • Servings = 6 • Calories = 145 • Total fat = <1 gm. • Cholesterol = 0 mg. • Sodium = 5 mg. • Total carbohydrate = 38 gm. • Dietary fiber = 1 gm. • Protein = <1 gm.

EXCHANGE VALUES—2 bread/starch

HAPPINESS IS. . .

SHRIMPY CUCUMBER MINT SANDWICHES

1 cucumber, peeled, thinly sliced
1/4 tsp. salt
1/2 cup mini shrimp, thawed
2 tsp. finely chopped fresh mint
1/4 tsp. sugar
1/4 tsp. lemon juice
3 Tbsp. low-fat margarine
4 slices whole wheat or white bread, crusts removed
1/2 tsp. white pepper
Sprigs of fresh mint (for garnish)
Thinly sliced cucumbers (for garnish)

Place cucumber slices in a bowl; sprinkle with salt. Allow to stand for 10 minutes, stirring once. Transfer to a colander and press out extra juice. Let drain for 15 minutes. Pat cucumber slices dry on paper towels. In a small bowl, mix shrimp, mint, sugar, lemon juice, and margarine until soft and creamy. Spread on bread. Arrange cucumbers on two of the slices of bread with spread. Season with pepper and top with the other slice of bread. Cut in squares. Arrange on white paper doily around edge of plate. Arrange additional sliced cucumbers in middle of plate. Lay long stems of fresh mint over cucumbers. *Preparation time = 25 minutes.*

NUTRITION FACTS—Serving size = 1/4 of a double slice sandwich
Servings = 8 • Calories = 90 • Total fat = 3 gm. • Cholesterol = 14 mg. • Sodium = 184 mg. • Total carbohydrate = 13 gm. • Dietary fiber = <1 gm. • Protein = 3 gm.

EXCHANGE VALUES—1/2 bread/starch, 1/2 vegetable, 1/2 fat

Mother's or Father's Day Shopping List

Take this book along to your supermarket or photocopy the list. Select the same number or size of items that you have in the past, based on the number of people for whom you are shopping. Review this list before you go to the store. Cross out items you have on hand, and write in your personal likes and needs.

Produce

Fresh strawberries
Onion
Green pepper
Sweet yellow pepper
Cucumber
Fresh mint
Kiwi

Packaged

Quick-cooking tapioca
Vanilla pudding

Staples/Spices

Olive oil
Chili powder
Flour
Salt
Sugar
Black pepper
White pepper
Cinnamon
Cornstarch
Nonfat cooking spray

Bottled/Canned

Low-salt tomatoes
Lemon juice
Mandarin orange sections
Apple cider

Frozen Case

Low-calorie whipped topping
Frozen strawberries
Mini shrimp
Frozen blueberries
Belgian waffles
Orange juice

Happiness Is. . .

REFRIGERATOR CASE

Low-fat margarine
Skim milk

MEAT CASE

Boneless, skinless
   chicken breasts

BAKERY/DELI

Whole wheat or white bread
Bread sticks

Romance Is in the Air

My son James helped name this chapter. Not bad for a 16 year old! Vibrant flowers decorate the table, glowing candles light the room, and a heart-shaped chocolate cake is waiting to be cut. It's a day to honor the love in your life. Enjoy!

Whether you're celebrating an anniversary, Valentine's Day, or another special romantic occasion, it can be an exciting time not only for the two of you, but for the entire family.

Even though you may want to take time to celebrate your relationship alone, it's important to include your children in the festivities and food. They'll be thrilled to share part of the day with you.

Romance Is in the Air Activities

1. Review the suggested menu items. You may want to personalize them with your favorite foods.

2. Make breakfast in bed complete with a bouquet of flowers or a special gift.

3. Later in the day, you may want to look through photo albums together and talk about why this relationship is so special.

Romance Is in the Air Menu

Dinner for Two—Made by the Children

* Zucchini Linguini
  Lettuce Salad
  Fat-Free Italian Vinaigrette
  Swedish Rye Bread

* Spicy Jello Parfait
  Coffee or Tea
  Skim Milk

Happiness Is. . .

Lovers' Patio Breakfast

* Overnight Cinnamon French Toast for Two
  Microwaved Canadian Bacon
  Fresh-Squeezed Orange Juice

* Red Hot Cinnamon Applesauce
  Skim Milk
  Maple Nut Coffee

Romantic Picnic for Two

Croissant With Deli Sandwich Filling
Low-Fat Deli Dill Weed Dip
Fresh Carrots, Broccoli, and Radishes

Low-Fat Cake Mix With Low-Fat Frosting
Beverages of Choice

(* recipe follows)

Dinner for Two Recipes

ZUCCHINI LINGUINI

1/3 lb. linguini (or spaghetti)
1 clove garlic, minced (or 1 tsp. crushed garlic)
2 green onions, chopped
1 large (or 2 small) zucchini, thinly sliced
4-oz. can mushrooms (or 1/4 lb. fresh, sliced)
2 Tbsp. low-fat margarine
2 or 3 medium tomatoes, chopped
2 Tbsp. chopped parsley
2 tsp. fresh basil, chopped (or 1/2 tsp. dried leaf)
1/2 tsp. salt
1/4 tsp. pepper
1/2 cup (or 4-oz. package) shredded mozzarella
3 Tbsp. Parmesan cheese

In a large saucepan (3 quarts or larger), bring water to boil. Add linguini and cook until done (about 10 to 12 minutes). In the meantime, sauté garlic, onions, zucchini, and mushrooms in margarine for 3 to 4 minutes. Add tomatoes, parsley, basil, salt, and pepper; simmer another 3 to 4 minutes. Combine vegetable mixture and linguini, then add mozzarella cheese. Mix gently. Sprinkle Parmesan cheese on top and serve immediately. *Preparation time = 30 minutes.*

NUTRITION FACTS—Serving size = 1 cup • Servings = 6 • Calories = 154 • Total fat = 6 gm. • Cholesterol = 13 mg. • Sodium 355 mg. • Total carbohydrate = 17 mg. • Dietary Fiber = 2 mg. • Protein = 9 gm.

EXCHANGE VALUES—1 bread/starch, 1 vegetable, 1 fat.

HAPPINESS IS. . .

Spicy Jello Parfait

11-oz. can mandarin oranges
3-oz. package sugar-free orange Jello
1/4 tsp. cardamom
1/2 tsp. cinnamon
1/4 tsp. ginger
1 cup nonfat plain yogurt

Prepare Jello using 1 cup liquid. Add spices to hot Jello and fold in yogurt. Drain mandarin oranges and add to the mixture. Pour into gelatin mold. Refrigerate for at least 1 hour. *Preparation time = 15 minutes. Refrigeration time = 60 minutes.*

NUTRITION FACTS—Serving size = 1/2 cup • Servings = 6 • Calories = 49 • Total fat = <1 gm. • Cholesterol = 4 mg. • Sodium = 32 mg. • Total carbohydrate = 7 gm. • Dietary fiber = 0 • Protein = 3 gm.

EXCHANGE VALUES—1/2 bread/starch, 1/2 vegetable

Lovers' Patio Breakfast Recipes

OVERNIGHT CINNAMON FRENCH TOAST FOR TWO

1 Tbsp. low-calorie maple syrup
2 Tbsp. low-fat margarine
1/4 cup brown sugar
4 slices split-top wheat bread
2 eggs (or 1/2 cup liquid egg substitute)
3/4 cup skim milk
1/2 tsp. vanilla
1/2 tsp. cinnamon
1/4 tsp. salt
1/2 cup pecans, broken
Nonstick cooking spray

Preheat oven to 350°. Prepare an 8" x 8" cake pan by spraying sides of pan with nonstick cooking spray. Combine syrup, margarine, brown sugar, and pecans and heat in microwave for 2 minutes. Spread mixture evenly over bottom of prepared pan. Place bread on top, two layers high. Beat eggs. Add skim milk, vanilla, cinnamon, and salt to eggs. Pour over bread. May be made the night before and refrigerated. Bake uncovered for 30 minutes. *Preparation time = 10 minutes. Baking time = 30 minutes.*

NUTRITION FACTS—Serving size = 1/2 piece • Servings = 4 • Calories = 292 • Total fat - 16 gm. • Cholesterol (with egg) = 107 mg. • Cholesterol (with egg substitute) = 1 mg. • Sodium = 383 mg. • Total carbohydrate = 31 gm. • Dietary fiber = 2 gm. • Protein = 8 gm.

EXCHANGE VALUES—2 bread/starch, 1 medium fat meat, 1 1/2 fat

HAPPINESS IS. . .

RED HOT CINNAMON APPLESAUCE

> 4 cups apples, peeled and sliced (tart apples used for pies are best)
> 1/2 cup water
> 3 tsp. cinnamon candies
> 4 Tbsp. sugar

Combine all ingredients in a saucepan, and cook for 5 to 10 minutes or until apples are soft. Cool and serve. *Stove-top preparation time = 20 minutes.*

Microwave method: Place all ingredients in a microwave-safe dish. Microwave on high for 5 minutes or until apples are soft. *Microwave preparation time = 15 minutes.*

NUTRITION FACTS—Serving size = 1/2 cup • Servings = 4 • Calories = 193 • Total fat = <1 gm. • Cholesterol = 0 mg. • Sodium = 261 mg. • Total carbohydrate = 50 gm. • Dietary fiber = 4 gm. • Protein = <1 gm.

EXCHANGE VALUES—2 1/2 bread/starch

NOTE: THIS RECIPE MAY NOT BE SUITABLE FOR INDIVIDUALS WITH ELEVATED BLOOD SUGAR OR TRIGLYCERIDES.

Romance Is in the Air Shopping List

Take this book along to your supermarket or photocopy the list. Select the same number or size of items that you have in the past, based on the number of people for whom you are shopping. Review this list before you go to the store. Cross out items you have on hand, and write in your personal likes and needs.

Produce

Broccoli
Carrots
Radishes
Garlic
Green onions
Zucchini
Tomatoes
Oranges (for fresh-squeezed orange juice)
Lettuce
Apples

Bottled/Canned

Nonfat mayonnaise
Mushrooms
Nonfat Italian vinaigrette
Mandarin oranges
Low-calorie maple syrup

Packaged

Cinnamon candies
Linguini
Sugar-free orange Jello
1/2 c. pecans
Maple nut coffee
Coffee
Tea
Low-fat cake mix
Parmesan cheese

Staples/Spices

Parsley
Basil
Salt
Pepper
Cardamom
Cinnamon
Ginger
Brown sugar
Vanilla
Sugar
Nonstick cooking spray

Happiness Is. . .

Meat Case

Canadian bacon

Refrigerator Case

Low-fat margarine
Shredded mozzarella or provolone
Nonfat plain yogurt
Eggs or egg substitute
Skim milk

Bakery/Deli

Swedish rye bread
Split-top wheat bread
Croissants
Deli sandwich filling of your choice (for croissants)
Low-fat deli dill weed dip

Creating Holiday Traditions

New Year's Resolutions
•
Ghosts & Goblins
•
Chestnuts Roasting by the Fire Weekend

New Year's Resolutions

It's the time to learn from years passed, create a new pathway in our lives, and set achievable goals for ourselves and our families. There will never be a better time to do it than during the new year.

This is a common time for people to make positive changes in their lives, to take time out to think about what they want to accomplish during the next year. For families, it's an especially good time to talk about goals they share together.

We've found it helpful to sit down and brainstorm about enjoyable ways we can spend time together and about other goals we want to accomplish. As we do this, we write down everyone's suggestions, decide on the goals for the year, and set a day to complete each one. After we've done this, we indulge in a delicious, simple meal together.

As time passes, it's common for goals to change, too. The importance isn't in meeting every goal, but in having goals to work toward. In a few weeks, we like to touch base and talk about whether any goals need to be refined or changed.

New Year's Resolutions Activities

1. Choose a day or evening before New Year's Day to have your first family brainstorming session. You may want to combine one of the meals for the New Year's theme with a brainstorming session.

2. Tape several pieces of paper together to make an "ideas board." Then write down everything that everyone suggests.

3. Prepare an informal meal, and encourage grazing or buffet-style dining. Family members can help themselves when they are hungry.

4. Distribute a copy of your "Family Resolutions" to each family member. This is a great time to take a family picture. Post this picture and your resolutions on the refrigerator.

5. Determine a tentative date to regroup and measure the success of your family goals. This date may change, but continue to keep the goals posted to encourage family members to continue working toward their resolutions.

New Year's Resolutions Menus

New Year's Eve Open House

* Spicy Smokie Links
* Muffin Quiches
* A Portrait of Fruit
* Annie's Fruit Dip
* Hot Wassail

New Year's Brunch

* Goulash
* Mardi Gras Salad
  Rainbow Sherbet
Skim Milk
Coffee or Tea

New Year's Soup Supper

* Tangy Broccoli Soup
  Low-Fat Sliced Ham Sandwiches
* New Year's Resolutions Cake
Skim Milk
Coffee or Tea

(* recipe follows)

New Year's Eve Open House Recipes

SPICY SMOKIE LINKS

12-oz. bottle chili sauce
10-oz. jar grape jelly
2 lb. low-fat miniature smokie links (smoked sausage made with turkey, pork, or beef)

Heat chili sauce and grape jelly in a saucepan until jelly is melted. Stir in smokie links. Simmer uncovered 30 minutes. Serve in a dish that can be kept warm, such as a fondue pot or chafing dish. *Preparation time = 10 minutes. Cooking time = 30 minutes.*

NUTRITION FACTS—Serving size = 3 links • Servings = 32 • Calories = 95 • Total fat = 4 gm. • Cholesterol = 8 mg. • Sodium = 466 mg. • Total carbohydrate = 12 gm. • Dietary fiber = <1 gm. • Protein = 4 gm.

EXCHANGE VALUES—1 bread/starch, 1/2 fat

MUFFIN QUICHES

1 cup part-skim mozzarella cheese, shredded
1/2 cup low-fat cheddar cheese, shredded
1/4 cup minced onion
4-oz. can mushrooms, drained
1/2 cup chopped broccoli
1 3/4 cups skim milk
4 eggs (or 1 cup liquid egg substitute)
1/2 cup reduced-fat Bisquick baking mix
1/4 tsp. salt
1/4 tsp. pepper
3 or 4 drops Tabasco sauce
Nutmeg (for garnish)
Nonstick cooking spray

Preheat oven to 350°. Combine cheeses, onion, mushrooms, and broccoli in mixing bowl; set aside. Combine milk, eggs, baking mix, salt, pepper, and Tabasco sauce in mixing bowl. Beat at high speed for 1 minute. Pour over cheese mixture. Using a measuring cup, ladle mixture into a cupcake pans sprayed with nonstick cooking spray. Bake 20-25 minutes. *Preparation time = 20 minutes. Baking time = 25 minutes*

NUTRITION FACTS—Serving size = 1 muffin quiche • Servings = 36 • Calories = 162 • Total fat = <1 gm. • Cholesterol (with egg) = 24 mg. • Cholesterol (with egg substitute) = <1 mg. • Sodium = 663 mg. • Total carbohydrate = 8 gm. • Dietary fiber = <1 gm. • Protein = 30 gm.

EXCHANGE VALUES—3 lean meat, 1/2 skim milk, 1 vegetable

A PORTRAIT OF FRUIT

Each Saturday and Sunday morning at the Parson's Inn, we create a picture of fruit, just like an artist. We serve our guests a large platter of fresh fruit arranged on ruffly lettuce. (You can encourage your children to help with this. Teach them that the platter is the artist's canvas, and each design is unique.)

> 1 lb. red or black grapes
> 3 bananas
> 2 kiwi
> 1 pineapple
> 2 red apples
> 1 bunch green leafy lettuce
>   (or any seasonal variety)

When pineapple is in season, use it as the centerpiece. Cut off the top and place it at one end of an oval platter on a liner of lettuce. Cut the body of the pineapple in two. Using a paring knife, cut out the fresh pineapple, removing the fibrous spikes and center. Cube pineapple and place in the two pineapple halves. Arrange these on the leafy lettuce. Remember, you are painting a picture.

Wash the grapes. Remove half the grapes from their stems, and cut in half. Place these grapes in the pineapple halves. Wash the apples and kiwi. Slice apples and remove the core, leaving the peel on. Cut into thin slices keeping the cut surface on the cutting board. Place one-fourth of the apple slices in pineapple halves. Peel and slice bananas. Place in pineapple halves. Slice kiwi with skin on. Arrange on platter with sliced apples. Complete your "portrait of fruit" with sprigs of grapes. Serve with Annie's Fruit Dip (on next page). *Preparation time = 15 to 30 minutes.*

NUTRITION FACTS—Serving size = 1 cup • Servings = 10 • Calories = 101 • Total fat = <1 gm. • Cholesterol = 0 mg. • Sodium = 2 mg. • Total carbohydrate = 26 gm. • Dietary fiber = 2 gm. • Protein = 1 gm.

EXCHANGE VALUES—2 fruit

ANNIE'S FRUIT DIP

This recipe is featured in 366 Low-Fat Brand-Name Recipes *by M.J. Smith. Annie is my beautiful daughter.*

> *3 oz. nonfat cream cheese*
> *7 oz. marshmallow creme*
> *1/4 tsp. lemon extract*
> *2 drops red food coloring*
> *4 cups prepared fresh fruit for dipping, such as pears, apples, oranges, grapes, and bananas*

Place cream cheese and marshmallow creme in a mixing bowl. Microwave on 50% power for 2 minutes. Stir. Heat again for 2 minutes. Continue stirring until smooth. Fold in lemon extract and food coloring, then transfer to a serving bowl. Refrigerate until serving time. Prepare assorted fresh fruits for dipping. Soak bananas, apples, and pears in chilled orange juice to prevent browning. Provide toothpicks for fruit dippers. *Preparation time = 15 minutes.*

NUTRITION FACTS—Serving size = 1/2 cup fruit + 1/8 cup dip • Servings = 8 • Calories = 154 • Total fat =1 gm. • Cholesterol = 2 mg. • Sodium = 31 mg. • Total carbohydrate = 39 gm. • Dietary fiber = 2 gm. • Protein = 1 gm.

EXCHANGE VALUES—2 1/2 fruit

HOT WASSAIL

4 cups unsweetened apple juice
3 cups unsweetened pineapple juice
2 cups cranberry juice cocktail
1/4 tsp. ground nutmeg
1 cinnamon stick
3 whole cloves
Lemon slices

Combine all ingredients in a large kettle and simmer for 10 minutes. Serve hot. *Preparation time = 10 minutes. Cooking time = 10 minutes.*

NUTRITION FACTS—Serving size = 1/2 cup • Servings = 18 • Calories = 67 • Total fat = <1 gm. • Cholesterol = 0 mg. • Sodium = 3 mg. • Total carbohydrate = 17 gm. • Dietary fiber = 0 gm. • Protein = <1 gm.

EXCHANGE VALUES—1 fruit

New Year's Brunch Recipes

GOULASH

1 cup minced onion
2 cloves garlic, minced
2 tsp. canola oil
1 lb. ground beef (97% nonfat)
13-oz. can cooked tomatoes (3 1/2 cups)
1 Tbsp. minced fresh parsley
2 tsp. Worcestershire sauce
2 tsp. brown sugar
1 tsp. salt
1/4 tsp. pepper
16 oz. macaroni, cooked
Grated Parmesan cheese (optional)

Sauté onion and garlic in oil until onions are transparent. Add ground beef and cook until browned. Add remaining ingredients except macaroni and cheese. Simmer slowly for 1 hour. Pour over hot macaroni on a serving platter. Sprinkle with grated Parmesan cheese if desired. *Preparation time = 20 minutes. Cooking time = 1 hour.*

NUTRITION FACTS—Serving size = 1 cup • Servings = 8 • Calories = 257 • Total fat = 10 gm. • Cholesterol = 49 mg. • Sodium = 580 mg. • Total carbohydrate = 23 gm. • Dietary fiber = 1 gm. • Protein = 18 gm.

EXCHANGE VALUES—1 1/2 bread/starch, 2 lean meat, 1 vegetable

MARDI GRAS SALAD

3 cups cooked colored rotini pasta
1/2 cup lean ham or turkey ham, cubed
15-oz. can red kidney beans, drained
1 cup carrots, sliced
1 cup broccoli, cut into small pieces
2 cups low-fat farmer's cheese, cubed
1 cup onion, chopped
1/2 cup nonfat Italian Dressing
Red onion rings

Cook pasta, then cool by running cold water over the pasta and drain well. Set aside. Combine the remaining ingredients, except dressing and onion rings, in a large bowl. Mix in the dressing. Garnish with onion rings. Refrigerate for at least an hour. *Preparation time = 30 minutes. Refrigeration time = 1 hour.*

NUTRITION FACTS—Serving size = 1/2 cup • Servings = 16 • Calories = 183 • Total fat = 4 gm. • Cholesterol = 18 mg. • Sodium = 122 mg. • Total carbohydrate = 16 gm. • Dietary fiber = 1 gm. • Protein = 10 gm.

EXCHANGE VALUES—1 bread/starch, 1 medium fat meat, 1 vegetable

New Year's Soup Supper Recipes

TANGY BROCCOLI SOUP

1/2 cup chopped onion
1/2 cup chopped green pepper
4 cups chopped fresh broccoli
4 Tbsp. low-fat margarine
3 cups low-sodium chicken broth
2 cups skim milk
1/2 cup flour
1/2 tsp. crushed red pepper
1 cup grated nonfat cheddar cheese
1 cup grated mozzarella cheese

In a 4 quart saucepan, sauté the onion, green pepper, and broccoli in margarine for 5 to 7 minutes or until tender. Add the chicken broth. Simmer for 30 minutes. Blend the milk and flour in a shaker container. Add milk to the saucepan, and stir until smooth. Add crushed pepper and the cheeses. Heat until the cheeses melts, stirring often. *Preparation time = 45 minutes.*

NUTRITION FACTS—Serving size = 1/2 cup • Servings = 12 • Calories = 149 • Total fat = 6 gm. • Cholesterol = 11 mg. • Sodium = 404 mg. • Total carbohydrate = 12 gm. • Dietary fiber = 2 gm. • Protein = 13 gm.

EXCHANGE VALUES—1 bread/starch, 1 lean meat, 1 vegetable

NEW YEAR'S RESOLUTIONS CAKE

1 low-fat white cake mix
6 Tbsp. creme de menthe
Green food coloring
16-oz. can low-fat fudge topping
12 oz. low-fat whipped topping

Prepare the cake mix as directed. Add 3 tablespoons creme de menthe and a few drops of green food coloring to batter. Bake and cool. Frost with fudge topping. Mix together whipped topping, 3 tablespoons creme de menthe, and a few drops of green food coloring. Spread on cake. Refrigerate. *Cake preparation time = 15 minutes. Frosting time = 15 minutes.*

NUTRITION FACTS—Serving size = 1/12 cake • Servings = 12 • Calories = 239 • Total fat = 8 gm. • Cholesterol = 4 mg. • Sodium = 8 mg. • Total carbohydrate = 54 gm. • Dietary fiber = 0 gm. • Protein = 3 gm.

EXCHANGE VALUES—2 1/2 bread/starch, 1 fat

NOTE: THIS RECIPE MAY NOT BE SUITABLE FOR INDIVIDUALS WITH ELEVATED BLOOD SUGAR OR TRIGLYCERIDES.

New Year's Resolutions Shopping List

Take this book along to your supermarket or photocopy the list. Select the same number or size of items that you have in the past, based on the number of people for whom you are shopping. Review this list before you go to the store. Cross out items you have on hand, and write in your personal likes and needs.

Produce

Fresh parsley
Garlic
Onions
Red onion
Green pepper
Broccoli
Carrots
Lettuce
Fresh fruit for fruit dip
Lemon
Red or Black Grapes
Bananas
Pineapple
Red apples
Kiwi

Packaged

Tea
Coffee
Reduced-fat Bisquick baking mix
Macaroni
Parmesan cheese
Colored rotini pasta
Low-fat white cake mix

Staples/Spices

Flour
Canola oil
Pepper
Salt
Lemon extract
Nutmeg
Red and green food coloring
Brown sugar
Cinnamon stick
Chopped pepper
Whole cloves
Crushed red pepper
Green food coloring

Bottled/Canned

Tomatoes
Kidney beans
Nonfat Italian dressing
Worcestershire sauce
"Lite" fudge topping
Mushrooms
Low-sodium chicken broth
Marshmallow creme
Chili sauce
Grape jelly
Cranberry juice
Unsweetened apple juice
Unsweetened pineapple juice

Frozen Case

Rainbow sherbet
Low-fat whiped topping

Refrigerator Case

Margarine
Skim milk
Nonfat cheddar cheese
Nonfat mozzarella cheese
Nonfat cream cheese
Eggs (or egg substitute)
Low-fat farmer's cheese

Meat Case

Low-fat miniature smokie links
97% nonfat ground beef
Lean ham or turkey ham

Bakery/Deli

Low-fat sliced ham sandwiches

Other

Creme de menthe

Ghosts and Goblins

The harvest moon shines high in the sky, pumpkins appear on every doorstep, and people of all ages are dressed in masks and capes. There's a good chance it's Halloween.

This holiday is a family favorite that both children and adults can take part in and enjoy. The costumes, face paint, masks, and bags full of treats are all part of the fun.

During the weekend, there's time to enjoy your favorite fare with the ghosts and goblins. The menu suggestions in this section are made to be fun and easy. Be creative and spontaneous, and have a spooktacular weekend together!

Ghosts and Goblins Activities

1. Assign teams to help develop characters, costumes, and silly masks. Include a song fest if family members play musical instruments.

2. Decide on a menu. Assign food preparation and grocery shopping tasks.

3. Line up board games for family and friends to play together.

4. Carve pumpkins or paint silly faces on them with markers. If you've carved your pumpkin, take out the seeds and roast them in the oven. Then make a pumpkin pie.

Ghosts and Goblins Menu

Jack-o-Lantern Lunch

* Avocado Pita-Witch
* Tangy Pears
  Skim Milk

Halloween Breakfast

* Pumpkin Pancakes
* Apple Raisin Compote
  Orange Juice

Trick-or-Treat Halloween Party

* Zucchini Lasagna   Halloween Cupcakes
* Dill Cheese Bread   Skim Milk
  Fresh Fruit

(* recipe follows)

Jack-O-Lantern Lunch Recipes

AVOCADO PITA-WITCH

4 pita pockets (14 oz. package)
2/3 cup nonfat mayonnaise
1 medium avocado
1/2 cup shredded mozzarella cheese (2 oz.)
1 medium tomato, chopped
4 Tbsp. shredded carrot
2 Tbsp. medium salsa
1 tsp. crushed garlic
1 tsp. cilantro

Cut pita bread in half. Spread mayonnaise inside of each pocket. Peel and seed avocado, then cut into chunks. Combine with cheese, tomato, carrot, salsa, garlic, and cilantro. Spoon into pita pockets. *Preparation time = 10 minutes.*

NUTRITION FACTS—Serving size = 1/2 pita pocket • Servings = 8 • Calories = 188 • Total fat = 7 gm. • Cholesterol = 11 mg. • Sodium = 499 mg. • Total carbohydrate = 25 gm. • Dietary fiber = 1 gm. • Protein = 6 gm.

EXCHANGE VALUES—2 bread/starch, 1 fat

TANGY PEARS

3 cups pears in light syrup
2 cups pink or red grapefruit juice
6 maraschino cherries
6 Tbsp. low-fat whipped topping
6 lettuce leaves

Drain pears and marinate in grapefruit juice for at least an hour. Place a pear half on each lettuce leaf, garnish with whipped topping, and top with a maraschino cherry. *Preparation time = 5 minutes. Marinating time = 1 hour.*

NUTRITION FACTS—Serving size = 1/2 pear • Servings = 6 • Calories = 128 • Total fat = 4 gm. • Cholesterol = 0 mg. • Sodium = 59 mg. • Total carbohydrate = 17 gm. • Dietary fiber = 1 gm. • Protein = 6 gm.

EXCHANGE VALUES—1 1/2 fruit, 1 fat

Halloween Breakfast Recipes

PUMPKIN PANCAKES

> 1 egg (or 1/4 cup liquid egg substitute)
> 1 cup skim milk
> 1/2 cup cooked or canned pumpkin
> 1 1/2 cups flour
> 1 tsp. baking powder
> 1 Tbsp. brown sugar
> 1/2 tsp. ground cinnamon
> 1/8 tsp. ground nutmeg
> 1/8 tsp. ground ginger
> 2 Tbsp. canola oil
> 1/2 cup chopped pecans
> Nonstick cooking spray

Combine all ingredients in a mixing bowl and stir just until blended. Pour the batter onto a hot griddle that has been lightly sprayed with nonstick cooking spray. Flip the pancakes over when slightly browned. Serve hot with Apple Raisin Compote (recipe is on next page). *Preparation time = 10 minutes.*

NUTRITION FACTS—Serving size = 2 pancakes • Servings = 6 • Calories = 259 • Total fat – 12 gm. • Cholesterol (with egg) = 18 mg. • Cholesterol (with egg substitute) = <1 mg. • Sodium = 58 mg. • Total carbohydrate = 31 gm. • Dietary fiber = 2 gm. • Protein = 7 gm.

EXCHANGE VALUES—2 bread/starch, 2 fat

APPLE RAISIN COMPOTE

1/2 cup raisins
2 cups applesauce
1/4 cup sugar
1 tsp. cinnamon

Cook raisins in 1 cup of water in microwave for 3 minutes. Drain and cool. In the meantime, combine applesauce, sugar, and cinnamon. Fold in raisins. This is good with pancakes. *Preparation time = 10 minutes. Cooking time = 3 minutes.*

NUTRITION FACTS—Serving size = 1/2 cup • Servings = 5 • Calories = 129 • Total fat = 4 gm. • Cholesterol = 0 mg. • Sodium = 4 mg. • Total carbohydrate = 34 gm. • Dietary fiber = 2 gm. • Protein = 1 gm.

EXCHANGE VALUES—2 fruit

Trick-or-Treat Halloween Party Recipes

ZUCCHINI LASAGNA

This is one of the recipes featured in M.J. Smith's All American Low-Fat Meals in Minutes. *I have served it to the hospital board of trustees, where it garnered great smiles of approval.*

1 lb. lean ground beef
1/2 cup onion, chopped
1/2 cup green pepper, chopped
4 oz. mushrooms, sliced
1/2 tsp. canola oil
4 small zucchini, peeled and sliced thin lengthwise
8 oz. no-salt tomato sauce
1/4 tsp. garlic powder
1/2 tsp. fennel
1/2 tsp. black pepper
1 tsp. basil
1 tsp. oregano
2 oz. mozzarella cheese, shredded
2/3 cup low-fat cottage cheese
1/3 cup Parmesan cheese
Nonstick cooking spray

Preheat oven to 375°. Brown and drain meat. Sauté onion, pepper, and mushrooms in oil in a Dutch oven or microwave 4 minutes in a 2-quart casserole dish. Meanwhile, steam the sliced zucchini 6 minutes on the stove top or microwave 3 minutes to steam in a covered container. Stir meat, tomato sauce, and seasonings into onion, pepper, mushroom mixture. Combine mozzarella cheese and cottage cheese in a separate container. Spray an 8" x 8" baking dish with nonstick cooking spray. Layer zucchini, cheese, meat sauce, zucchini, cheese, meat sauce, and repeat. Sprinkle Parmesan cheese over top of the last meat layer. Bake 45 minutes or microwave 20 to 25 minutes. This can be assembled and frozen for later use. *Preparation time = 15 minutes. Baking time = 45 minutes. Microwave cooking time = 25 minutes.*

NUTRITION FACTS—Serving size = 1 1/2 cups • Servings = 4 • Calories = 298 • Total fat = 9 gm. • Cholesterol = 77 mg. • Sodium = 421 mg. • Total carbohydrate = 22 gm. • Dietary fiber = 4 gm. • Protein = 33 gm.

EXCHANGE VALUES—3 lean meat, 1 skim milk, 2 vegetable

DILL CHEESE BREAD

1 pkg. dry yeast
1/4 cup warm water
1 cup skim milk
4 Tbsp. tub margarine
3 1/2 to 4 cups flour
2 Tbsp. sugar
1 tsp. salt
1 Tbsp. dillweed
1 tsp. garlic powder
1 egg, beaten (or 1/4 cup liquid egg substitute)
2 Tbsp. butter, melted
2 Tbsp. grated Parmesan cheese
Nonstick cooking spray

Preheat oven to 400°. Sprinkle yeast in 1/4 cup warm water and let dissolve for 10 minutes. Combine and heat milk and margarine; heat only until margarine melts. Add egg. Do not boil. Then let cool. In large mixing bowl, combine flour, sugar, salt, dillweed, and garlic powder. Set aside. Combine yeast and milk-margarine mixture. Gradually add to flour mixture, mixing well. Dough should be soft but not sticky. Add another tablespoon of flour if necessary. Place dough on a floured bread board and knead 3 to 4 minutes.

Spray bowl and bread pans with nonstick cooking spray. Place dough in a greased bowl. Cover and let rise until double in bulk. Punch down. Cover and let rise until it doubles in size again. Punch down and shape into greased round loaf pan or 2 greased bread pans. Drizzle melted butter over top and sprinkle with grated cheese. Cover and let rise to double in bulk. Bake 25 to 30 minutes until golden brown. *Preparation time – 2 1/2 hours. Baking time = 25 to 30 minutes.*

NUTRITION FACTS—Serving size = 1 slice • Servings = 20 • Calories = 116 • Total fat = 2 gm. • Cholesterol (with egg) = 11 mg. • Cholesterol (with egg substitute) = <1 mg. • Sodium = 157 mg. • Total carbohydrate = 20 gm. • Dietary fiber = <1 gm. • Protein = 3 gm.

EXCHANGE VALUES—1 bread/starch, 1 vegetable

Ghosts and Goblins Shopping List

Take this book along to your supermarket or photocopy the list. Select the same number or size of items that you have in the past, based on the number of people for whom you are shopping. Review this list before you go to the store. Cross out items you have on hand, and write in your personal likes and needs.

Produce

Avocado
Tomato
Carrots
Lettuce
Cilantro
Garlic
Zucchini
Onion
Pepper
Mushrooms

Packaged

Parmesan cheese
Dry yeast
Raisins
Chopped pecans

Staples/Spices

Cinnamon
Flour
Salt
Dill Weed

Garlic powder
Baking powder
Sugar
Brown sugar
Nutmeg
Ginger
Basil
Oregano
Pepper
Canola oil
Fennel
Nonstick cooking spray

Bottled/Canned

No-salt tomato sauce
Pink or red grapefruit juice
Salsa
Applesauce
Pumpkin
Pears in light syrup
Maraschino cherries

Frozen Case

Orange juice
Low-fat whipped topping

Refrigerator Case

Nonfat mayonnaise
Shredded mozzarella
Skim milk
Low-fat margarine
Eggs (or egg substitute)
Low-fat cottage cheese

Meat Case

Lean ground beef

Bakery/Deli

Pita pockets
Halloween cupcakes

Chestnuts Roasting by the Fire

Snow covers every inch of the ground; family and friends are together, and aromas from the kitchen bring a smile to everyone in the room. The holidays are a joyous time!

This time of year is celebrated in many different ways. Some people choose to carry on family traditions from past generations; others combine old ways with traditions of their own.

However you decide to spend your holiday, it's important to share it with people who are important in your life. This section includes special entrees and desserts that everyone can indulge in and enjoy.

Chestnuts Roasting by the Fire Activities

1. Encourage children to make handmade gifts that express their creativity, talents, and love.

2. Consider delivering plates of sweets or hot meals on Christmas Eve or Christmas Day to elderly couples in your neighborhood. Your children can get in on the act, too.

3. Organize cookie baking parties, holiday recipe swaps, and Christmas wrapping bees. Holiday music helps set the mood.

4. Sharing holiday chores can enhance the spirit of sharing and heighten the festive atmosphere as friends gather

    Examples of chores to share are cleaning the spare bedroom where guests will stay; baking cookies or making candy; wrapping presents; shopping together; and decorating the house.

5. Discuss realistic gift expectations with your children during the holidays. Begin early by limiting their gifts to what is appropriate for your budget.

6. Spend quality time with your children; just relax or play a new board game.

7. Design menus that encourage family members to help.

8. Mix, roll, and bake cookies weeks before Christmas. Store in tightly covered containers or foil-lined coffee cans so they are ready when carolers call.

8. Delegate all food-related tasks, including cleanup. It will help if everyone takes part in the cleanup so the games and cards can begin.

CHESTNUTS ROASTING BY THE FIRE MENUS

HOLIDAY DECORATING BRUNCH

* Herbal Spinach Chicken Lasagna

　Pomegranate

* Garlic Bread

* Jolly Gelatin Snowman

　Skim Milk

CHRISTMAS COOKIE PARTY EXCHANGE

* Rolled Sugar Cookies
* Gingerbread Cookies
* Eggnog

* Mom's Thumbprint Jams

TRADITIONAL HOLIDAY DINNER

* Traditional Roasted Turkey or
  * Microwaved Boneless Turkey
* Low-Salt, Low-Fat Pan Gravy
* Sage Dressing
* Whole Wheat Rolls
* Riced Potatoes
* Orange-Cheese Dressing

* Molded Cranberry Salad

　Assorted Cookie Plate

　Coffee or Tea

　Non-Alcoholic Wine

　Skim Milk

(* recipe follows)

Holiday Decorating Brunch Recipes

HERBAL SPINACH CHICKEN LASAGNA

10-oz. box frozen chopped spinach
16 oz. low-fat ricotta cheese
2 cups cooked chicken, chopped
2 cups (or 1 15-oz. jar) spaghetti sauce
8 oz. low-fat mozzarella cheese, sliced
1 Tbsp. fresh basil, minced
1 tsp. fresh fennel (chop only the heads)
Fresh fennel (for garnish)
Nonstick cooking spray
1/4 cup grated Parmesan cheese

Preheat oven to 350°. Thaw the spinach and squeeze dry. Put about 1/3 of the spinach in the bottom of a casserole dish that has been sprayed with nonstick cooking spray. Spread half of the ricotta over the spinach. Put half of the chicken on the ricotta. Spoon on half of the spaghetti sauce. Top with half of the mozzarella slices. Sprinkle on half of the basil and fennel. Repeat the layering process, using another third of the spinach then the rest of the ricotta, chicken, spaghetti sauce, and mozzarella. Finish with the final third of spinach. Sprinkle on the Parmesan cheese with the rest of the basil and fennel. *Preparation time = 10 minutes. Baking time = 45 minutes.*

NUTRITION FACTS—Serving size = 3/4 cup • Servings = 12 • Calories = 231 • Total fat = 12 gm. • Cholesterol = 25 mg. • Sodium = 609 mg. • Total carbohydrate = 12 gm. • Dietary fiber = 0 • Protein = 20 gm.

EXCHANGE VALUES—1 bread/starch, 2 medium fat meat

JOLLY GELATIN SNOWMAN

3 cups boiling water
1 cinnamon stick
3 packages (4-serving size)
  sugar-free raspberry flavor gelatin
2 cups apple juice

Bring water and cinnamon stick to boil in a medium saucepan. Pour over gelatin in a large bowl; dissolve gelatin completely. Stir in apple juice. Remove cinnamon stick. Spray snowman or 6-cup mold with nonstick cooking spray. Pour gelatin into mold. Refrigerate at least 4 hours or until firm. To unmold, dip mold in hot water 10 to 15 seconds. Gently pull gelatin from around edges with moist fingers. Place moistened serving plate on top of mold. Invert and shake lightly to loosen. Gently remove mold.

Possible decorations include whipped topping, cinnamon sticks, sliced fruit, or whole cloves. *Preparation time = 15 minutes. Setting time = 4 hours.*

NUTRITION FACTS—Serving size = 1/2 cup • Servings = 10 • Calories = 32 • Total fat = 0 gm. • Cholesterol = 0 mg. • Sodium = 66 mg. • Total carbohydrate = 7 gm. • Dietary fiber = 0 gm. • Protein = 2 gm.

EXCHANGE VALUES—1/2 bread/starch

GARLIC BREAD

1 medium size loaf French bread
1/3 cup low-fat margarine
1/4 tsp. garlic powder

Preheat oven to 350°. Cut the French bread into slices, but do not slice all the way through the crust; leave the bottom crust intact. Melt the margarine and mix in the garlic powder. With a pastry brush, spread the margarine on both sides of the bread slices. (Other herbs that could be used are basil, marjoram, and oregano.) Wrap the loaf tightly in foil. Place in the oven until bread is lightly browned, about 20 minutes. *Preparation time = 15 minutes. Baking time = 20 minutes.*

NUTRITION FACTS—Serving size = 1 slice • Servings = 12 • Calories = 54 • Total fat = 5 gm. • Cholesterol = 0 mg. • Sodium = 109 mg. • Total carbohydrate = 2 gm. • Dietary fiber = <1 gm. • Protein = <1 gm.

EXCHANGE VALUES—1 bread/starch

Christmas Cookie Party Exchange Recipes

ROLLED SUGAR COOKIES

1/2 cup low-fat margarine
1/2 cup sugar
1 tsp. pure vanilla extract (or 2 tsp. of imitation)
1 egg (or 1/4 cup liquid egg substitute)
2 cups flour
1 tsp. baking soda
1 tsp. salt
1/2 tsp. nutmeg

Preheat oven to 350°. Cream together the margarine, sugar, vanilla, and egg until light and fluffy. Add the flour and spices. Blend until well mixed. Chill the dough for 2 hours or overnight. Roll out on a lightly floured surface until 1/8 inch thick. Cut with a cookie cutter. Sprinkle with red or green sugar. Place on a nonstick baking sheet. Bake about 10 minutes or until lightly browned. Cool before storing. *Preparation time = 15 minutes. Baking time = 10 minutes.*

NUTRITION FACTS—Serving size = 1 cookie • Servings = 36 cookies • Calories = 49 • Total fat = 1 gm. • Cholesterol (with egg) = 6 mg. • Cholesterol (with egg substitute) = 0 • Sodium = 120 mg. • Total carbohydrate = 8 gm. • Dietary fiber = <1 gm. • Protein = 1.5 gm.

EXCHANGE VALUES—1/2 bread/starch

GINGERBREAD COOKIES

1/2 cup sugar
1/2 cup low-fat margarine
1/2 cup molasses
1 egg (or 1/4 cup liquid egg substitute)
1 tsp. lemon extract
1 tsp. baking soda dissolved in 2 Tbsp. flour
1 tsp. cinnamon
1 tsp. ginger
2 1/2 to 3 cups flour

Preheat oven to 350°. Combine sugar, margarine, molasses, egg, and lemon extract in a bowl; blend with mixer. In a separate bowl, combine dry ingredients and add to first mixture. Mix thoroughly. Refrigerate 1 hour before rolling out. Roll out on a lightly floured surface to 1/8-inch thick. Cut with gingerbread man cookie cutter and place on a nonstick cookie sheet. Bake 8 to 10 minutes until cookies are firm to the touch and slightly brown on the edges. Cool and decorate as desired. *Preparation time = 15 minutes. Baking time = 10 minutes.*

NUTRITION FACTS—Serving size = 1 cookie • Servings = 14 • Calories = 179 • Total fat = 4 gm. • Cholesterol (with egg) = 15 mg. • Cholesterol (with egg substitute) = 0 mg. • Sodium = 153 mg. • Total carbohydrate = 34 gm. • Dietary fiber = <1 gm. • Protein = 3 gm.

EXCHANGE VALUES—2 bread/starch, 1/2 fat

MOM'S THUMBPRINT JAMS

1 cup low-fat margarine
2/3 cup sugar
1 egg (or 1/4 cup liquid egg substitute)
1/2 tsp. vanilla
1/2 tsp. salt
2 cups flour
1 egg (or 1/4 cup egg substitute)
1 cup chopped walnuts or pecans
1 cup natural fruit spread
Nonstick cooking spray

Preheat oven to 350°. Cream margarine and sugar; blend in egg and vanilla. Sift in dry ingredients. Chill dough for 2 or more hours. Roll dough into walnut-sized balls, dip in egg (or egg substitute), and roll in nuts. Place balls on a baking sheet, sprayed with nonstick cooking spray. Make a thumbprint in each; fill each indentation with fruit spread. Bake for 15 to 18 minutes. *Preparation time = 10 minutes. Refrigeration time = 2 hours. Baking time = 18 minutes.*

NUTRITION FACTS—Serving size = 1 cookie • Servings = 36 • Calories = 125 • Total fat = 5 gm. • Cholesterol (with egg) = 12 mg. • Cholesterol (with egg substitute) = 0 mg. • Sodium = 79 mg. • Total carbohydrate = 16 gm. • Dietary fiber = <1 gm. • Protein = 2 gm.

EXCHANGE VALUES—1 bread/starch, 1 fat

EGGNOG

1/2 cup liquid egg substitute
4 cups skim milk
2 egg whites
1 tsp. vanilla
1/2 cup sugar
1/2 tsp. brandy or rum flavoring
Ground nutmeg

Combine egg substitute and milk in a saucepan. Cook over medium heat until the mixture coats a metal spoon. Cool. In a separate bowl, beat egg whites until soft peaks form. Fold into the egg mixture. Add the vanilla, sugar, and flavoring. Cover and chill. Pour into serving cups and garnish with nutmeg. *Preparation time = 30 minutes.*

NUTRITION FACTS—Serving size = 1/2 cup • Servings = 6 • Calories = 134 • Total fat = <1 gm. • Cholesterol = 3 mg. • Sodium = 136 mg. • Total carbohydrate = 25 gm. • Dietary fiber = 0 gm. • Protein = 8 gm.

EXCHANGE VALUES—1 bread/starch, 1 lean meat

Traditional Holiday Dinner Recipes

TRADITIONAL ROASTED TURKEY

If turkey is frozen, thaw in the refrigerator. This may take one to three days, depending upon the size of the turkey. Once the turkey is thoroughly thawed, wash it with cold water, inside and out. Pat dry. Rub cavities with seasonings such as sage.

Stuff turkey just before roasting. Stuff wishbone cavity lightly and skewer to back. Spoon remaining stuffing into the large cavity. Shake bird to settle stuffing; do not pack. Close the opening by placing skewers across it and lacing shut with string. Tie drumsticks securely to the tail. Grease skin thoroughly with low-fat margarine. Insert meat thermometer in the center of the inside thigh muscle. Make sure the thermometer is not touching the bone.

Place the turkey in a roasting pan breast side up. Cover loosely with aluminum foil, pressing it lightly at drumstick and breast ends. Roast at a constant low temperature of 325°. When the turkey is about two-thirds done, according to the roasting chart, cut the string holding the thighs so heat can reach inside. About 20 minutes before roasting time is finished, press thick part of drumstick between fingers (protect hand with paper towel). If the bird is done, the meat will feel very soft and the drumstick will move easily or even twist out of joint. (Your meat thermometer should register 190° to 195°.) Let turkey stand 20 minutes before carving. *Preparation time = 30 minutes. Cooking time = see chart on next page.*

NUTRITION FACTS—Serving size = 4 oz. • Servings = 2 servings per lb. • Calories = 212 • Total fat = 4 gm. (without skin) • Cholesterol = 83 mg. • Sodium = 70 mg. • Total carbohydrate = 0 gm. • Dietary fiber = 0 gm. • Protein = 30 gm.

EXCHANGE VALUES—4 lean meat

Cooking Chart for Whole Turkey

Ready-to-cook weight (before stuffing)

8 TO 12 LBS. . . . . 4 TO 4 1/2 HRS.

12 TO 16 LBS. . . . . 4 1/2 TO 5 1/2 HRS.

16 TO 20 LBS. . . . . 5 1/2 TO 7 HRS.

MICROWAVED BONELESS TURKEY BREAST

Place a 4 to 5 pound turkey breast in a microwave-safe dish, skin side down. Cover and microwave on high for 10 minutes. Turn down to half power and cook for 40 to 50 minutes, pausing halfway through the cooking time to the turn breast over. A microwave meat thermometer should register 170°. Let stand 10 minutes before carving. *Preparation time = 10 minutes. Cooking time = 60 minutes. Resting time = 10 minutes.*

NUTRITION FACTS—Serving size = 3.5 oz. • Servings = 20 • Calories = 212 • Total fat = 8 gm. • Cholesterol = 83 mg. • Sodium = 70 mg. • Total carbohydrate = 0 gm. • Dietary fiber = 0 gm. • Protein = 32 gm.

EXCHANGE VALUES—4 lean meat

SAGE DRESSING

1/2 cup low-fat margarine
1 cup minced onion
1 cup minced celery
8 cups dry bread cubes
1 tsp. dry sage or 1 Tbsp. chopped fresh sage
3/4 tsp. salt
1/2 tsp. pepper
4 to 6 cups of poultry broth to moisten

Preheat oven to 350°. Sauté onion and celery in margarine. Add bread cubes, seasonings, and poultry broth. Toss gently to mix. This dressing can be baked for an hour or used as stuffing for poultry. Allow 3/4 to 1 cup stuffing for each pound of poultry. (Note: Stuffing will be very moist.) *Preparation time = 15 minutes. Baking time = 1 hour.*

NUTRITION FACTS—Serving size = 1/2 cup • Servings = 10 • Calories = 222 • Total fat = 7 gm. • Cholesterol = <1 mg. • Sodium = 693 mg. • Total carbohydrate = 34 gm. • Dietary fiber = 2 gm. • Protein = 6 gm.

EXCHANGE VALUES—2 bread/starch, 1 fat

RICED POTATOES

6 medium potatoes, peeled
1/2 tsp. salt
White pepper to taste (optional)

Cut potatoes into chunks, and place in a saucepan. Cover with water. Add salt. Boil 15 to 20 minutes until soft when tested with a fork. Put potatoes through a ricer. *Preparation time = 15 minutes. Cooking time = 20 minutes.*

NUTRITION FACTS—Serving size = 3/4 cup • Servings = 4 • Calories = 174 • Total fat = <1 gm. • Cholesterol = 0 mg. • Sodium = 277 mg. • Total carbohydrate = 41 gm. • Dietary fiber = 3 gm. • Protein = 3 gm.

EXCHANGE VALUES—2 bread/starch

LOW-SALT, LOW-FAT PAN GRAVY

12 ice cubes
2 cups liquid turkey stock
3 Tbsp. flour, heaping

Remove turkey from roasting pan, and place ice cubes in drippings. Fat will adhere to ice cubes. Remove ice cubes and discard fat. Measure liquid into roasting pan; stir and scrape all brown drippings loose from pan. Heat mixture. Mix flour with a small amount of water until smooth. Add flour mixture to remainder of turkey stock roasting pan. Cook over medium heat, stirring steadily until it is bubbling. *Preparation time = 15 minutes.*

NUTRITION FACTS—Serving size = 3 Tbsp. • Servings = 16 • Calories = 37 • Total fat = 3 gm. • Cholesterol = 2 mg. • Sodium = 197 mg. • Total carbohydrate = 1 gm. • Dietary fiber = <1 gm. • Protein = 2 gm.

EXCHANGE VALUES—1 fat

MOLDED CRANBERRY SALAD

2 6-oz. packages sugar-free
   strawberry flavored gelatin
5 medium oranges
16-oz. package cranberries
1 cup sugar
Nonstick cooking spray

In a large bowl, dissolve gelatin in 3 cups of boiling water. Stir in 3 cups of cold water. Refrigerate, stirring occasionally, until mixture is slightly thickened.

Meanwhile, peel and chop oranges; place in another large bowl. Coarsely chop the cranberries. Mix cranberries and sugar, stirring until sugar is completely dissolved. Stir fruit mixture into slightly thickened gelatin. Pour into a Bundt pan or 12-cup mold sprayed with nonstick cooking spray. Refrigerate until set.

To unmold, dip in hot water for 10 to 15 seconds. Place a moistened serving plate on top of the mold. Shake slightly and gently remove the mold. Garnish with Orange-Cheese dressing (recipe on the next page). *Preparation time = 30 minutes. Refrigeration time = 2 hours.*

NUTRITION FACTS—Serving size = 1/2 cup • Servings = 16 • Calories = 16 • Total fat = <1 gm. • Cholesterol = 0 mg. • Sodium = 41 mg. • Total carbohydrate = 19 gm. • Dietary fiber = 1 gm. • Protein = 1 gm.

EXCHANGE VALUES—1 vegetable

ORANGE-CHEESE DRESSING

8-oz. package fat-free cream cheese
1/3 cup orange juice
2 tsp. grated orange peel

Beat cream cheese and orange juice with a mixer at low speed until smooth. Stir in orange peel. Serve with molded cranberry salad (recipe on previous page). *Preparation time = 10 minutes.*

NUTRITION FACTS—Serving size = 1 Tbsp. • Servings = 16 • Calories = 32 • Total fat = 3 gm. • Cholesterol = 5 mg. • Sodium = 80 mg. • Total carbohydrate = 1 gm. • Dietary fiber = 0 gm. • Protein = 2 gm.

EXCHANGE VALUES—1/2 fat

WHOLE WHEAT ROLLS

> 2 packages active dry yeast
> 1/2 cup lukewarm water (110°)
> 1 cup warm skim milk, warm (110°)
> 1/4 cup low-fat margarine
> 1 cup instant potato flakes
> 1/4 cup brown sugar
> 1 tsp. salt
> 2 eggs or 1/2 cup liquid egg substitute
> 2 cups whole wheat flour
> 2 cups all purpose flour

In a small bowl, dissolve yeast in lukewarm water. In a large mixing bowl, combine warm milk, margarine, potato flakes, brown sugar, and salt. Cool the mixture to lukewarm. Add yeast mixture, eggs, and whole wheat flour to milk mixture. Beat until smooth using an electric mixer. Stir in enough of the all purpose flour to make a soft dough.

Knead on a floured surface until smooth and elastic. Place in a greased bowl. Grease the top of the dough lightly. Place in a warm spot and let rise until doubled, about an hour. Punch dough down. Shape dough into 2-inch balls and place them, barely touching each other, in greased baking pans. Cover and let rise until double in size. Bake rolls in a preheated 375° oven 15 to 20 minutes until golden brown. Remove rolls from pan to a cooling rack. *Preparation time = 30 minutes. Rising time = 2 hours. Baking time = 20 minutes.*

NUTRITION FACTS—Serving size = 1 roll • Servings = 36 • Calories = 76 • Total fat = 2 gm. • Cholesterol (with egg) = 13 mg. • Cholesterol (with egg substitute) = 1 mg. • Sodium = 107 mg. • Total carbohydrate = 13 gm. • Dietary fiber = 1 gm. • Protein = 2 gm.

EXCHANGE VALUES—1 bread/starch

Chestnuts Roasting by the Fire Shopping List

Take this book along to your supermarket or photocopy the list. Select the same number or size of items that you have in the past, based on the number of people for whom you are shopping. Review this list before you go to the store. Cross out items that you have on hand. Write in your personal likes and needs.

Produce

Onions
Celery
Pomegranates
Potatoes
Oranges
Cranberries
Basil, fresh
Fennel, fresh

Packaged

Bread cubes
Walnuts or pecans
Parmesan cheese
Instant potato flakes
Sugar-free raspberry gelatin
Sugar-free strawberry gelatin
Active dry yeast
Coffee
Tea

Staples/Spices

Cinnamon
Ginger
Vanilla
Baking powder
Salt
Nutmeg
Black Pepper
White pepper
Garlic powder
Sugar
Brown sugar
Baking soda
White flour
Whole wheat flour
Lemon extract
Sage
Cinnamon stick
Grated orange peel
Brandy or rum flavoring
Nonstick cooking spray

Bottled/Canned

Natural fruit spread
Spaghetti sauce
Molasses
Apple juice
Low-sodium chicken bouillon

Frozen Case

Frozen, chopped spinach
Orange juice

Refrigerator Case

Low-fat ricotta cheese
Low-fat mozzarella cheese
Low-fat margarine
Eggs or egg substitute
Skim milk
Fat-free cream cheese

Meat Case

Boneless chicken breasts
Boneless turkey breast or
  12-18 lb. turkey

Bakery/Deli

French bread

Just for Fun

HOLLYWOOD FAVORITES
•
RELAXING AT THE BEACH
•
PIZZA & CARDS
•
RAINY DAY COMFORT

HOLLYWOOD FAVORITES

The screen is flickering with action and everyone's intently watching the adventures of their favorite actor. Meanwhile, a delicious dinner is being prepared. We can't wait to taste the conclusion; could it be death by chocolate?

Once in a while, it's fun to spend a weekend watching everyone's favorite Hollywood movie. It's a time to compare favorite actors and actresses and just plain have fun.

This section has great recipes to enjoy during a movie-goer's weekend. We hope you like what you see!

HOLLYWOOD FAVORITES ACTIVITIES

1. Write five questions to stump family members about your favorite movies and stars.

2. Choose the actors and actresses you expect to win this year's Oscar and Emmy awards. Place everyone's choices in a sealed envelope. Find out how many winners you picked at a gathering after the awards have been presented.

3. Pick a movie to see together—and have a great time!

Hollywood Favorites Menus

Oscar Day Brunch

* Creamy Cucumber Soup
  Toasted Bagels
* Orange Chicken
  Salad Almondine

Yogurt
Soft Drinks
Coffee or Tea

Lunch on the Set

* Eggplant Fiesta
* Movie "Star" Fruit Plate
* Orange Burst Fruit Dip

Crusty Hard Rolls
Skim Milk
Soft Drinks

Rodeo Drive Dinner

* Star Studded Salmon Patties
* Tomato Steaks
  Lettuce Salad
  Choice of Dressing

* Rock Star Brownies
  Skim Milk
  Coffee or Tea

(* recipe follows)

Just for Fun

Oscar Day Brunch Recipes

CREAMY CUCUMBER SOUP

1 cup skim milk
8-oz. carton nonfat sour cream
8-oz. carton low-fat plain yogurt
2 cucumbers, peeled, seeded, and chopped
1 green onion, chopped
1 Tbsp. minced fresh dillweed
1 Tbsp. lemon juice
1/2 tsp. salt
1/4 tsp. white pepper
Dash of hot sauce
Optional garnish: dillweed sprigs

Combine all ingredients except garnish in a blender or food processor. Cover and process just until smooth. Chill thoroughly. Stir well before serving. Garnish with dillweed. *Preparation time = 30 minutes. Refrigeration time = 60 minutes.*

NUTRITION FACTS—Serving size = 1 cup • Servings = 4 • Calories = 115 • Total fat = <1 gm. • Cholesterol = 2 mg. • Sodium = 402 mg. • Total carbohydrates = 21 gm. • Dietary fiber = 3 gm. • Protein = 11 gm. •

EXCHANGE VALUES—1 bread/starch, 1/2 skim milk

ORANGE CHICKEN SALAD ALMONDINE

1 pkg. Good Seasons Zesty Herb fat-free dressing
1/4 cup white vinegar
1/2 cup frozen orange juice concentrate
2 tsp. sugar
1 head romaine lettuce
2 celery stalks
2 green onions
2 oz. sliced almonds
1 1/2 tsp. canola oil
1 1/2 tsp. low-fat margarine
2 6-oz. skinless chicken breasts
Lawry's lemon pepper seasoning
12 oz. can mandarin oranges

Preheat oven to 350°. Combine Zesty Herb mix with white vinegar and orange juice concentrate. (When adding water to concentrate, use 2/3 amount of water required.) Stir in sugar. Refrigerate for at least 3 hours. Cut romaine lettuce into bite-size pieces. Chop celery and onions and add to lettuce. Refrigerate. Sauté sliced almonds in oil and margarine until lightly browned. Baste chicken breasts with orange juice and sprinkle with lemon pepper seasoning to taste. Bake breasts for 30 minutes. Cool and dice into 1/2-inch sections. Add ingredients to salad greens just before serving to prevent the lettuce from wilting. Arrange greens on plate. Add 3 ounces mandarin oranges, 2 tablespoons almonds, and 3 ounces diced chicken breast. Ladle 2 1/2 ounces dressing on top and serve. *Preparation time = 30 minutes. Refrigeration time = 3 hours. Baking time = 30 minutes.*

NUTRITION FACTS—Serving size = 3 oz. chicken • Servings = 4 • Calories = 380 • Total fat = 19 gm. • Cholesterol = 81 mg. • Sodium = 223 mg. • Total carbohydrates = 21 gm. • Dietary fiber = 5 gm. • Protein = 32 gm.

EXCHANGE VALUES—4 lean meat, 1/2 bread/starch, 2 fat

Lunch on the Set Recipes

EGGPLANT FIESTA

3/4 lb. ground round or extra lean ground beef
1 medium eggplant (1 1/2 lbs.)
1 small onion, chopped
1 medium fresh ginger root, chopped
1 medium orange
1/4 cup cider vinegar
1 Tbsp. lemon juice
1 tsp. crushed garlic in oil
1/2 tsp. basil
1/2 tsp. marjoram
1/4 cup seedless raisins
2 Tbsp. low-calorie pancake syrup
2 eggs (or 1/2 cup egg substitute)
1/4 cup grated Parmesan cheese
Endive for garnish

Preheat oven to 350°. Microwave ground beef on high power until brown. Drain. Crumble meat into small pieces. Wash eggplant in cool water and pat dry. Slice eggplant in half. Carve out inside meat with a sharp knife. Cut meat into cubes and save shell halves for stuffing. (Note: to remove bitter taste from eggplant, salt flesh and place in water between two soup bowls, with a weight on top. Let sit for 30 minutes, then drain away accumulated bitter-tasting liquid. Wash eggplant meat in colander to remove added salt).

Add 2 to 3 cups of water to eggplant, cover, and microwave on high power for 5 minutes. Drain off liquid. Place onion in a blender with 1 cup of water and chop. Drain; measure 2 tablespoons, and set aside. Place ginger in blender with 1 cup water and chop. Drain, measure 1 tablespoon, and set aside. Discard rest onion and ginger.

Peel orange, break into sections, and remove white skin. Cut sections in 1/4-inch pieces, and place in a pan. Add 1 tablespoon ginger, 2 tablespoons onion, vinegar, lemon juice, garlic, basil, marjoram, raisins, and syrup. Cook slowly over low heat for 5 to 10 minutes, stirring often, until pulp softens. Set aside to cool.

Combine eggs, browned ground meat, eggplant, and pulp mixture in a bowl. Spoon mixture into eggplant shells. Sprinkle with Parmesan cheese and bake for 50 to 60 minutes. Allow eggplant to set for 5 minutes before serving. Serve over leafy endive. *Preparation time = 30 minutes. Baking time = 60 minutes.*

NUTRITION FACTS—Serving size = 3/4 cup • Servings = 6 • Calories 246 = • Total fat = 11 gm. • Cholesterol (with egg) = 127 mg. • Cholesterol (with egg substitute) = 56 mg. • Sodium = 111 mg. • Total carbohydrates = 17 gm. • Dietary fiber = 4 gm. • Protein = 20 gm.

EXCHANGE VALUES—1 bread/starch, 1 vegetable, 1 lean meat, 2 fat

MOVIE "STAR" FRUIT PLATE

2 star fruit
1 lb. red or black grapes
4 kiwi
2 yellow Delicious apples
1 bunch red leafy lettuce
4 bananas

Wash the star fruit, grapes, kiwi, and apples; set aside. Wash the lettuce with cold water. Pat dry with a towel to add crispness. Place the lettuce on a platter. Slice the star fruit, and place in the middle of the platter. Slice the kiwi and bananas, and cube the apples, then place the fruit around the star fruit. Cut the grapes into small bunches, and place them around the platter. *Preparation time = 25 minutes.*

NUTRITION FACTS—Serving size = 1 cup • Servings = 10 • Calories = 101 • Total fat = <1 gm. • Cholesterol = 0 mg. • Sodium = 2 mg. • Total carbohydrates = 26 gm. • Dietary fiber = 2 gm. • Protein = 1 gm.

EXCHANGE VALUES—1/2 fruit

ORANGE BURST FRUIT DIP

1/4 cup sugar
1/4 cup orange juice
2 cups nonfat sour cream
1 Tbsp. orange peel, grated

In a small bowl, stir together all ingredients. Cover. Refrigerate at least 30 minutes. Serve with fruit plate. *Preparation time = 10 minutes. Refrigeration time = 30 minutes.*

NUTRITION FACTS—Serving size = 1/4 cup • Servings = 8 • Calories = 54 • Total fat = 0 gm. • Cholesterol = 0 mg. • Sodium = 40 mg. • Total carbohydrates = 12 gm. • Dietary fiber = 1 gm. • Protein = 3 gm.

EXCHANGE VALUES—1 bread/starch

Rodeo Drive Dinner Recipes

STAR STUDDED SALMON PATTIES

1 can (14-3/4 oz.) pink salmon
1/2 cup soda crackers, broken into pieces
1/2 cup chopped onion
1 cup finely chopped carrots
2 eggs (or 1/2 cup egg substitute)
1 tsp. tarragon
1/4 tsp. white pepper
1 tsp. crushed garlic
2 Tbsp. olive oil
1 can (10-3/4 oz.) Campbell's Healthy Request cream of celery soup
1/2 cup skim milk
2 Tbsp. chopped fresh basil
Nonstick cooking spray

Preheat oven to 300°. Combine salmon, crackers, onion, carrots, and eggs. Add tarragon, white pepper, and crushed garlic. Form into eight patties, and brown on both sides in olive oil in a nonstick pan. Heat together soup and milk until warm; add fresh basil to soup mixture. Put browned salmon patties in a casserole dish sprayed with nonstick cooking spray. Cover patties with soup mixture. Bake for 25 to 30 minutes, covered. If made ahead, bake for 30 to 35 minutes, covered. *Preparation time = 30 minutes. Baking time = 30 minutes.*

NUTRITION FACTS—Serving size = 1 patty • Servings = 8 • Calories = 133 • Total fat = 5 gm. • Cholesterol (with egg) = 54 mg. • Cholesterol (with egg substitute) = 1 mg. • Sodium = 475 mg. • Total carbohydrates = 7 gm. • Dietary fiber = <1 gm. • Protein = 14 gm.

EXCHANGE VALUES—2 lean meat, 1/2 fat

TOMATO STEAKS

2 medium, semi-ripe tomatoes
1/2 cup egg substitute
1/4 cup water
1/2 cup white flour
2 tsp. crushed garlic
1 tsp. Mrs. Dash® salt-free seasoning
1 tsp. Dijon mustard
5 tsp. olive oil

Wash tomatoes. Cut off and discard ends, and slice into 6 to 8 half-inch slices. Combine egg substitute and water. Add flour, garlic, seasoning, and mustard, and mix thoroughly. Place batter in a shallow dish and dip tomatoes in batter (use tongs to hold tomato slices). Set aside. Place olive oil in a 12-inch nonstick skillet. Heat to medium high. Add tomatoes, and cook, turning slices frequently, until slices are medium brown. Drain and pat tomatoes dry with paper towel. Garnish with parsley and serve. *Preparation time = 10 minutes. Cooking time = 15 minutes.*

NUTRITION FACTS—Serving size = 2 slices • Servings = 4 • Calories = 132 • Total fat = 5 gm. • Cholesterol = 0 • Sodium = 43 mg. • Total carbohydrates = 17 gm. • Dietary fiber = 0 • Protein = 5 gm.

EXCHANGE VALUES—1 bread/starch, 1 fat

ROCK STAR BROWNIES

1/2 cup unsweetened applesauce
1 cup sugar
1 tsp. cinnamon
2 egg whites
1/2 tsp. vanilla
3/4 cup flour
1/4 cup cocoa
1/4 tsp. baking powder
1/8 tsp. salt
Nonstick cooking spray

Preheat oven to 350°. Spray a 9" x 9" baking pan with nonstick cooking spray; set aside. In mixer bowl, combine applesauce, sugar, cinnamon, egg whites, and vanilla. Stir in flour, cocoa, baking powder, and salt. Pour into pan and bake for 20 to 25 minutes. *Preparation time = 15 minutes. Baking time = 25 minutes.*

NUTRITION FACTS—Serving size = 1 piece • Servings = 16 • Calories = 92 • Total fat = <1 gm. • Cholesterol = 0 mg. • Sodium = 35 mg. • Total carbohydrates = 20 gm. • Dietary fiber = <1 gm. • Protein = 2 gm.

EXCHANGE VALUES—1 bread/starch

Hollywood Favorites Shopping List

Take this book along to your supermarket or photocopy the list. Select the same number or size of items that you have in the past, based on the number of people for whom you are shopping. Review this list before you go to the store. Cross out items you have on hand, and write in your personal likes and needs.

Produce

Celery
Cucumbers
Onions
Green onions
Fresh dillweed
Carrots
Fresh basil
Semi-ripe tomatoes
Red leafy lettuce
Romaine lettuce
Eggplant
Fresh ginger root
Bananas
Yellow Delicious apples
Kiwi
Star fruit
Red or black grapes
Orange
Parsley

Packaged

Coffee
Tea
Good Seasons Zesty Herb fat-free dressing
Almonds
Soda crackers
Cocoa
Seedless raisins
Parmesan cheese

Staples/Spices

Salt
White pepper
Sugar
Canola oil
Lawry's lemon pepper seasoning
Tarragon
Garlic (crushed), in oil
Cinnamon
Vanilla
Flour
Baking powder
Salt-free seasoning
Olive oil
Basil
Marjoram
Orange peel (grated)

Bottled/Canned

Unsweetened applesauce
Dijon mustard
Lemon juice
Hot sauce
Mandarin oranges
White vinegar
Pink salmon
Campbell's Healthy Request
　cream of celery soup
Salad dressing
Cider vinegar
Reduced-calorie
　pancake syrup

Frozen Case

Orange juice

Refrigerator Case

Skim milk
Nonfat sour cream
Low-fat plain yogurt
Low-fat margarine
Eggs or egg substitute

Meat Case

Chicken breasts
Extra-lean ground beef

Bakery/Deli

Bagels
Crusty hard rolls

Other

Nonstick cooking spray
Soft drinks

Relaxing at the Beach

You dig your heels into the sand and make yourself comfortable for the lazy day ahead. As you lie there, the sun beats down and you can hear the waves gently rushing into shore. What a beautiful day to enjoy with family and friends.

A day at the beach can be a wonderful time to have fun with people you care about; and fun includes food. The dishes in this section can be prepared before you head out for the water.

Share a variety of scrumptious foods such as tortellini supreme, turkey cucumber pita pockets, and chocolate sandwiches for dessert. There's rarely a dull moment at the beach!

Relaxing at the Beach Activities

1. Keep summer afternoons less structured to take advantage of spontaneity.

2. Prepare quick and easy snacks for your next free afternoon. Designate a shelf in the pantry as well as one in the refrigerator and freezer for "low-fat snacks." Keeping these well stocked may speed up the packing-up process.

3. You may want to take an ecologically safe picnic. This means packing food in containers that can be rewashed, and using cloth napkins to save on waste.

4. Be sure to pack lots of sunscreen; apply regularly.

5. Try to anticipate what the children may need; a few extra bandages, tissues, and hair bands may save the day.

6. Bring favorite toys and sports equipment so everyone can have fun.

7. Sit back, relax, and enjoy!

Relaxing at the Beach Menus

Saturday Grazing

* Tortellini Supreme
* Parmesan Topped
  Corn on the Cob
  French Bread

Honeydew Melon
Skim Milk

Roadside Lunch

* Turkey Cucumber Pita Pockets
  Sliced Tomatoes
  Tapioca Pudding

Skim Milk
Soft Drinks

Sunday Picnic on the Beach

* Taco Salad
  Baked Low-Fat Tortilla Chips
  Watermelon Cubes

Green Seedless Grapes
Skim Milk
Drinks of Choice

Late Afternoon Snacks

* Chocolate Sandwiches
  Chunked Low-fat Turkey
  Ham and Low-fat Cheese

* Strawberry Ice

(* recipe follows)

Saturday Grazing Recipes

TORTELLINI SUPREME

>9 oz. pkg. cheese tortellini
>8 oz. fresh mushrooms, sliced
>1 green pepper, cut into strips
>1/2 cup chopped onions
>2 cloves garlic, minced (or 2 tsp. crushed garlic)
>1 Tbsp. olive oil
>1 1/2 cup Healthy Choice Italian-style vegetable pasta sauce
>1/2 cup water
>1 tsp. oregano
>1 tsp. basil

Cook tortellini according to directions. Drain. Sauté mushrooms, pepper, onions, and garlic in olive oil for about 5 minutes. Add pasta sauce, water, and spices, and cook over low heat for another 5 minutes. Add cooked, drained tortellini to pasta mixture, heating thoroughly. *Preparation time = 15 minutes. Cooking time = 15 minutes.*

NUTRITION FACTS—Serving size = 3/4 cup • Servings = 4 • Calories = 288 • Total fat = 9 gm. • Cholesterol = 23 mg. • Sodium = 613 mg. • Total carbohydrate = 41 gm. • Dietary fiber = 3 gm. • Protein = 12 gm.

EXCHANGE VALUES—3 starch/bread, 1 fat

PARMESAN TOPPED CORN ON THE COB

1 1/2 qt. water
4 ears sweet corn, husked and washed
1 Tbsp. Parmesan cheese
2 Tbsp. squeeze margarine

Bring water to boil in a 2-quart saucepan. Drop corn in the boiling water. Cover and cook 3 to 6 minutes, just until the milk in the kernels is set.

MICROWAVE METHOD—Microwave corn at full power in a plasctic bag with ears flat for 3 minutes. Turn bag over and microwave 3 more minutes. Let stand for 5 minutes. Drain and place on platter.

Squeeze on margarine and sprinkle with Parmesan cheese. *Preparation time = 10 minutes. Cooking time = 6 minutes. Standing time = 5 minutes.*

NUTRITION FACTS—Serving size = 1 ear of corn • Servings = 4 • Calories = 126 • Total fat = 7 gm. • Cholesterol = 4 mg. • Sodium = 102 mg. • Total carbohydrate = 14 gm. • Dietary fiber = 0 gm. • Protein = 4 gm.

EXCHANGE VALUES—1 bread/starch, 1 fat

Roadside Lunch Recipes

TURKEY CUCUMBER PITA POCKETS

1 lb. raw turkey breast slices (about 4 slices)
1 Tbsp. olive oil
1 cup diced cucumber
3/4 cup fresh chopped red pepper
4 Tbsp. low-fat mayonnaise
2 Tbsp. nonfat sour cream
1 tsp. onion powder
1 tsp. crushed garlic
2 tsp. dillweed
2 pita pockets, cut in half

Brown turkey slices in olive oil. Cut into thin strips. Add the rest of the ingredients, and mix well. Spoon into pita pocket halves. *Preparation time = 20 minutes.*

NUTRITION FACTS—Serving size = 1/2 pita pocket • Servings = 4 • Calories = 295 • Total fat = 5 gm. • Cholesterol = 95 mg. • Sodium = 420 mg. • Total carbohydrate = 24 gm. • Dietary fiber = 1 gm. • Protein = 38 gm.

EXCHANGE VALUES—4 lean meat, 1 bread/starch

Sunday Picnic on the Beach Recipes

TACO SALAD

1 head lettuce
1 lb. 97% fat-free ground beef
1/4-oz. package taco seasoning mix
15-oz. can kidney beans
1/2 cup onion, chopped
2 medium tomatoes, chopped
8-oz. nonfat Mexican-style shredded cheese
8-oz. bottle low-fat Western Mexican dressing
8-oz. low-fat baked tortilla chips, unsalted
Salsa and nonfat sour cream (optional)

Wash lettuce and cut into small pieces. Place in a 9" x 13" casserole or baking dish. Brown the ground beef, then add taco seasoning and cook according to directions on the package. Set the beef aside to cool. Drain kidney beans. Sprinkle the beans, cooled beef, chopped onions, chopped tomatoes, and cheese over the lettuce. Just before serving, pour dressing over salad. Serve with tortilla chips, salsa, and sour cream, if desired. *Preparation time = 30 minutes.*

NUTRITION FACTS—Serving size = 1 cup • Servings = 12 • Calories = 292 • Total fat = 9 gm. • Cholesterol = 35 mg. • Sodium = 631 mg. • Total carbohydrates = 33 gm. • Dietary fiber = 3 gm. • Protein = 19 gm.

EXCHANGE VALUES—2 bread/starch, 2 lean meat, 1 fat

Late Afternoon Snack Recipes

CHOCOLATE SANDWICHES

*3-oz. package instant sugar-free
  chocolate pudding*
1 cup skim milk
3/4 cup low-fat whipped topping
1 cup miniature marshmallows
*1 pkg. graham crackers
  (20 2-1/2-inch squares)*

Prepare pudding according to directions using only 1 cup skim milk. Add whipped topping and marshmallows. Spoon between graham crackers and freeze. *Preparation time = 10 minutes. Freezing time = 1 hour.*

NUTRITION FACTS—Serving size = 1 sandwich • Servings = 10 • Calories = 204 • Total fat = 2 gm. • Cholesterol = 3 mg. • Sodium = 136 mg. • Total carbohydrate = 44 gm. • Dietary fiber = 0 gm. • Protein = 3 gm.

EXCHANGE VALUES—2 1/2 bread/starch

STRAWBERRY ICE

2 cups fresh strawberries
4 ice cubes
1 tsp. dry lemonade mix (sugar-free Crystal Light can be substituted)

Wash and cut up strawberries. Mix ingredients together in blender until thick. Pour into glasses. Eat with a spoon. *Preparation time = 10 minutes.*

NUTRITION FACTS—Serving size = 1 cup • Servings = 2 • Calories = 109 • Total fat = 1 gm. • Cholesterol = 0 mg. • Sodium = 6 mg. • Total carbohydrate = 26 gm. • Dietary fiber = 8 gm. • Protein = 2 gm.

EXCHANGE VALUES—1 bread/starch, 1 fruit

Relaxing at the Beach Shopping List

Take this book along to your supermarket or photocopy the list. Select the same number or size of items that you have in the past, based on the number of people for whom you are shopping. Review this list before you go to the store. Cross out items that you have on hand, and write in your personal likes and needs.

Produce

Garlic cloves
Sweet corn
Fresh mushrooms
Green pepper
Red pepper
Onions
Cucumber
Strawberries
Honeydew melon
Lettuce
Tomatoes
Watermelon
Green seedless grapes

Packaged

Tapioca pudding
Instant sugar-free chocolate pudding
Taco seasoning mix
Dry lemonade mix
Miniature marshmallows
Graham crackers
Parmesan cheese

Staples/Spices

Oregano
Basil
Onion powder
Dillweed

Bottled/Canned

Olive oil
Healthy Choice Italian-style vegetable pasta sauce
Kidney beans
Low-fat Western Mexican dressing
Low-fat margarine

Frozen Case

Low-fat whipped topping

Refrigerator Case

Skim milk
Squeeze margarine
Cheese tortellini
Nonfat sour cream
Nonfat shredded Mexican-style cheese
Low-fat cheese

Meat Case

Low-fat turkey ham
97% fat-free ground beef
Raw turkey breast slices

Bakery/Deli

Pocket bread
French bread

Snack Foods

Baked low-fat tortilla chips, unsalted

Other

Soft drinks

Pizza and Cards

It's Saturday night and everyone is home. The fire is roaring and the family is looking forward to share the evening together; it's a perfect night for eating pizza and playing card games.

This kind of quality time doesn't come around often. But when it does, it's a wonderful way to enjoy games and good food together. Try delicious fruit pizza, chicken fajita pizza, or Hawaiian breakfast sandwich pizza.

Pizza and Cards Activities

1. Buy *Hoyle's Rules of Games*. Research a variety of card games suitable to the age groups of your family members.

2. Look over the pizza suggestions in this section. Add new and different recipes, or choose an old favorite.

3. Let everyone take part in making great-tasting pizzas.

4. Demonstrate how to clean, slice, and chop a variety of vegetables used in this chapter.

Pizza and Cards Menus

Pizza Brunch

* BLT Pizza
* Fruit Pizza
  Bread Sticks and Sauce

* Lemon Almond Cookies
  Skim Milk
  Soft Drinks

Pizza and Cards Supper

* Chicken Fajita Pizza
  Cheese Sauce
* Chocolate-Peanut Butter Pudding

* Cucumber Salad
  Nacho Chips

Pizza Breakfast

* Hawaiian Breakfast Sandwich Pizza
  Apple Juice
  Skim Milk

(* recipe follows)

Pizza Brunch Recipes

BLT PIZZA

>12-inch unbaked whole wheat pizza crust
>1 Tbsp. oregano
>1/2 tsp. cayenne pepper (optional)
>1/4 tsp. garlic powder
>4-oz. can no-salt-added tomato sauce
>3.5-oz. pkg. Canadian bacon, cut into pieces
>4 oz. nonfat shredded mozzarella cheese
>4 oz. nonfat shredded cheddar cheese
>1/2 cup nonfat mayonnaise
>1/2 tsp. paprika
>1/2 cup onion, chopped
>1/2 head lettuce, chopped into pieces
>2 medium tomatoes, chopped

Preheat oven to 450°. Prepare pizza crust according to directions on page XXX. Set aside. Mix oregano, cayenne pepper, and garlic powder into tomato sauce. Spread tomato sauce over crust. Arrange Canadian bacon pieces on sauce. Sprinkle with cheeses. Bake for 15 to 20 minutes. Cool for about 10 minutes. Cut into pieces. Combine mayonnaise, paprika, and onion. Spread over pizza. Layer lettuce and tomatoes on pizza. *Preparation time = 30 minutes. Baking time = 20 minutes.*

NUTRITION FACTS—Serving size: 1/12th of pizza • Servings =12 • Calories = 181 • Total fat = 3 gm. • Cholesterol = 9 mg. • Sodium = 519 mg. • Total carbohydrate = 30 gm. • Dietary fiber = 4 gm. • Protein = 11 gm.

EXCHANGE VALUES—2 bread/starch, 1 vegetable

FRUIT PIZZA

1/2 cup low-fat margarine
1/4 cup brown sugar
1 cup flour
1/4 cup quick-cooking oats
8-oz. pkg. nonfat cream cheese
1/3 cup brown sugar
1/2 tsp. vanilla
2 kiwi fruit, peeled and sliced
1 banana, peeled and chunked
1 pt. fresh blueberries
1 pt. fresh strawberries, sliced
8-oz. can crushed pineapple, drained
1/2 cup raspberry fruit spread
2 Tbsp. water
Nonstick cooking spray

Preheat oven to 375°. Spray a 12-inch pizza pan with nonstick cooking spray. In a small mixing bowl, cream together margarine, brown sugar, flour, and oats. Press dough onto the pizza pan. Prick dough with a fork. Bake for 10 to 12 minutes or until golden brown. Cool. Combine cream cheese, sugar, and vanilla. Blend well. Spread over crust. Arrange fruit attractively on cream cheese mixture. Combine fruit spread and water. Brush or drizzle mixture over fruit to form a glaze. Chill. Cut into wedges with a pizza cutter. *Preparation time = 30 minutes. Baking time = 12 minutes. Refrigeration time = 1 hour.*

NUTRITION FACTS—Serving size: 1/12th of pizza • Servings = 12 • Calories = 248 • Total fat = 11 gm. • Cholesterol = 21 mg. • Sodium = 129 mg. • Total carbohydrates = 37 gm. • Dietary fiber = 2 gm. • Protein = 3 gm.

EXCHANGE VALUES—1 1/2 bread/starch, 1 1/2 fruit, 1 1/2 fat

KATHY'S LEMON ALMOND COOKIES

Kathy and I made this recipe in high school home economics class along with a baked Alaska that almost slid off the plate! What fun and great memories. Kathy and Bill have raised two fine sons, and they all share my love of fine antiques.

> *1 cup all purpose flour*
> *1/2 cup low-fat margarine*
> *1/2 tsp. salt*
> *1/4 cup sugar*
> *1/2 tsp. lemon extract*
> *Nonstick cooking spray*
> *1 egg yolk (or 2 Tbsp. egg substitute)*
> *1 Tbsp. water*
> *1/4 cup blanched almonds*
> *Waxed paper*
> *Kitchen gloves*

Preheat oven to 400°. Place flour in a bowl and cut in margarine until texture is fine. Use gloved hands to work in salt, sugar, and lemon extract. Shape dough into a long roll, one-inch in diameter. Wrap in waxed paper, and chill about an hour. Cut roll into 1/4-inch slices. Place 1-inch apart on cookie sheet sprayed with nonstick cooking spray. Brush each slice with a mixture of egg yolk and water. Press 1/2 blanched almond piece into the top of each cookie. Bake 8 to 10 minutes or until light golden brown. *Preparation time = 15 minutes. Refrigeration time = 1 hour. Baking time = 10 minutes.*

NUTRITION FACTS—Serving size = 1 cookie • Servings = 24 cookies • Calories = 57 • Total fat = 3 gm. • Cholesterol (with real egg) = 9 mg. • Cholesterol (with egg substitute) = 0 • Sodium = 80 mg. • Total carbohydrates = 7 gm. • Dietary fiber = <1 gm. • Protein = 1 gm.

EXCHANGE VALUES—1/2 bread/starch, 1/2 fat

JUST FOR FUN

Pizza and Cards Supper Recipes

CHICKEN FAJITA PIZZA

12 inch whole wheat pizza crust
2 3-oz. boneless, skinless chicken breasts, sliced thin
1 tsp. crushed hot pepper
1 tsp. black pepper
1/2 cup mild salsa
8 oz. can tomato sauce
8 oz. fresh mushrooms, sliced
1 medium tomato, chunked
1 cup nonfat Mexican-style cheese
Nonstick cooking spray

Preheat oven to 450°. Prepare whole wheat pizza crust according to directions on page 10. Set aside. Roll chicken strips in mixture of hot pepper and black pepper, and brown in a skillet sprayed lightly with nonstick cooking spray. Mix salsa and tomato sauce together. Spread sauce evenly over pizza crust. Put chicken, mushrooms, tomatoes, and cheese on pizza. Bake for 15 minutes. Serve with additional crushed peppers to taste. *Preparation time = 30 minutes. Rising Time = 1 hour. Baking time = 15 minutes.*

NUTRITION FACTS—Serving size = 1/12 of pizza • Servings = 12 • Calories = 125 • Total fat = 1 gm. • Cholesterol = 12 mg. • Sodium = 267 mg. • Total carbohydrates = 18 gm. • Dietary fiber = 3 gm. • Protein = 10 gm.

EXCHANGE VALUES—1 bread/starch, 1/2 skim milk

CUCUMBER SALAD

3 medium cucumbers
3/4 cup red onion, sliced
1/2 tsp. salt
2 Tbsp. canola oil
1/2 cup cider vinegar
2 Tbsp. sugar
1/4 tsp. white pepper

Peel and slice cucumbers. Add onions and salt; stir well. Set aside for 15 minutes. Mix oil, vinegar, and sugar; pour over cucumber mixture. Add pepper. Marinate in refrigerator for an hour, stirring several times. Can be kept for three to four days. *Preparation time = 15 minutes. Refrigeration time = 60 minutes.*

NUTRITION FACTS—Serving size = 1/2 cup • Servings = 8 • Calories = 52 • Total fat = 4 gm. • Cholesterol = 0 mg. • Sodium = 135 mg. • Total carbohydrates = 10 gm. • Dietary fiber = 1 gm. • Protein = <1 gm.

EXCHANGE VALUES—1 vegetable, 1/2 fat

CHOCOLATE-PEANUT BUTTER PUDDING

2 cups skim milk
1/2 cup sugar
1/4 cup unsweetened cocoa powder
3 Tbsp. cornstarch
1 tsp. cinnamon
1/2 cup reduced-fat creamy peanut butter
1 tsp. vanilla
2 bananas, sliced

Combine milk, sugar, cocoa, cornstarch, and cinnamon in a medium saucepan. Cook on medium heat for about four to six minutes, stirring slowly. When pudding begins to thicken, add peanut butter and vanilla. Cook and stir two minutes more, or until thickened. Pour into a bowl. Cover, and chill. Serve in stemmed glasses or sauce dishes. Top each with several slices of banana. *Preparation time = 20 minutes. Refrigeration time = 30 minutes.*

NUTRITION FACTS—Serving size = 1/2 cup • Servings = 5 • Calories = 320 • Total fat = 10 gm. • Cholesterol = 2 mg. • Sodium = 204 mg. • Total carbohydrates = 51 mg. • Dietary fiber = 1 gm. • Protein = 11 gm.

EXCHANGE VALUES—2 bread/starch, 1 skim milk, 1 1/2 fat

Pizza Breakfast Recipes

HAWAIIAN BREAKFAST SANDWICH

> 12-inch loaf French bread
> 10 oz. farmer's cheese, grated
> 1/3 cup plain low-fat yogurt
> 1 Tbsp. honey mustard
> 6 oz. ham, sliced 1/2-inch thick
> 4 Tbsp. crushed pineapple, drained

Preheat oven to 350°. Cut bread in half lengthwise. Mix cheese, yogurt, and mustard together. Spread on lower half of bread. Arrange ham slices over cheese mixture, and spread pineapple over ham. Cover with top half of bread. Wrap in foil and bake 15 to 20 minutes. Cut into 2-inch slices and serve. *Preparation time = 15 minutes. Baking time = 20 minutes.*

NUTRITION FACTS—Serving size = 2-inch slice • Servings = 6 • Calories = 412 • Total fat = 9 gm. • Cholesterol = 31 mg. • Sodium = 1035 mg. • Total carbohydrates = 59 gm. • Dietary fiber = 3 gm. • Protein = 21 gm.

EXCHANGE VALUES—2 medium fat meat, 1 1/2 bread/starch, 1 skim milk, 1 fat

Pizza and Cards Shopping List

Take this book along to your supermarket or photocopy the list. Select the same number or size items that you have in the past, based on the number of people for whom you are shopping. Review this list before you go to the store. Cross out items you have on hand, and write in your personal likes and needs.

Produce

Kiwi
Mushrooms
Cucumbers
Onions
Green pepper
Red pepper
Bananas
Tomatoes
Lettuce
Strawberries
Blueberries
Red onion

Packaged

Quick-cooking oats
Unsweetened cocoa powder
Cornstarch
Dry yeast
Blanched almonds

Staples/Spices

Lemon extract
Oregano
Cayenne pepper
Garlic powder
Paprika
Salt
Sugar
Brown sugar
Black pepper
White pepper
Canola oil
Cinnamon
Vanilla
Crushed hot pepper
White flour
Whole wheat flour
Nonstick cooking spray

Bottled/Canned

Crushed pineapple
Pineapple tidbits
Cider Vinegar
Reduced-fat peanut butter
Mild salsa
No-salt tomato sauce
Apple juice
Nacho cheese sauce
Honey mustard

Raspberry fruit spread
Nonfat mayonnaise

REFRIGERATOR CASE

Skim milk
Mexican-style nonfat cheese
Low-fat margarine
Eggs or egg substitute
Nonfat cheddar cheese
Nonfat mozzarella cheese,
Nonfat cream cheese
Low-fat farmer's cheese
Plain nonfat yogurt

MEAT CASE

Chicken breasts
Canadian bacon
Ham slices

BAKERY/DELI

Soft bread sticks
12-inch French bread

SNACK FOODS

Nacho chips

OTHER

Soft drinks
Kitchen gloves
Waxed paper

Rainy Day Comfort

The weather is cold and damp, rain is pouring down in buckets, and everyone wants to stay inside and relax. What a day for a daydream!

A rainy day can be dreary, especially when it keeps you indoors for most of the day. But, depending on your family's interests, there are lots of relaxing activities and foods you can enjoy together.

Take time out of your relaxing schedule to indulge in some of the menu suggestions in this section. They're fun to make on days like these.

Rainy Day Comfort Activities

1. Escape the rain by reading your favorite book. Choose a comfortable place to enjoy this time; snuggle up with a cozy blanket and a hot drink.

2. Play games you haven't played for a while. Candyland, Chutes and Ladders, Rummy Royal, and War are some of our favorites.

3. Have an indoor picnic. Prepare sandwiches, salads, and other delicious foods to eat in a nontraditional location, like under the table.

4. Do something thoughtful for a loved one. Prepare Mom's bathroom with candles, scented bath water, classical music, and her favorite book or magazine. Set up Dad's recliner with a cup of hot cocoa, the remote control, and his favorite afghan.

5. Go outside to stomp and splash through the puddles just for fun. You'll feel like a kid again!

Rainy Day Comfort Menus

Curled Up With a Favorite Book

* Peg's Asparagus-Potato Soup   Soup Crackers
  Fresh Fruit   Beverage of Choice

Breakfast at Noon

* Brunch Style Potato Pancakes   Skim Milk
  Syrup   Coffee or Tea

Relaxing Fireside Supper

* Caesar's Chicken Salad   Coffee or Tea
* Microwave Cheese Potatoes   Skim Milk
  Hard Rolls
* M.J.'s Chocolate
  Zucchini Pound Cake

Curled Up With a Favorite Book Recipes

PEG'S ASPARAGUS-POTATO SOUP

1 can (13-3/4 oz.) low-salt chicken broth
3 medium potatoes, chopped
1/3 cup chopped onions
1/4 tsp. salt
1/4 tsp. nutmeg
8 oz. frozen asparagus
5 oz. nonfat cream cheese
1 1/2 cups skim milk

Combine chicken broth, potatoes, onions, salt, and nutmeg in a saucepan. Bring to a boil. Reduce heat, and simmer, covered, 5 to 8 minutes until potatoes just become tender. Add asparagus; return to a boil. Reduce heat and simmer 5 minutes or until vegetables are tender. Blend cream cheese and milk together, stirring into soup mixture until melted. DO NOT BOIL. *Preparation time = 30 minutes.*

NUTRITION FACTS—Serving size = 1 cup • Servings = 6 • Calories = 127 • Total fat = <1 gm. • Cholesterol = 4 mg. • Sodium = 445 mg. • Total carbohydrate = 22 gm. • Dietary fiber = <1 gm. • Protein = 9 gm.

EXCHANGE VALUES—1 1/2 bread/starch

Breakfast at Noon Recipes

BRUNCH-STYLE POTATO PANCAKES

4 medium potatoes, peeled and chunked
1 egg, beaten (or 1/4 cup egg substitute)
1/2 tsp. salt
1/4 tsp. pepper
1 cup nonfat shredded sharp cheddar cheese
2 Tbsp. finely chopped parsley
1 Tbsp. dried thyme
1/4 cup yellow cornmeal
Nonstick cooking spray

Boil potatoes until tender, about 15 minutes. Drain. Mash potatoes until quite smooth. Blend in egg, salt, and pepper. Add cheese, parsley, thyme, and 1 tablespoon of cornmeal. Form mixture into 8 oval patties about 3/4-inch thick. Roll in remaining cornmeal, coating completely. Spray a nonstick skillet with nonstick cooking spray. Fry patties until bottoms are golden, about 4 to 5 minutes. Turn patties over to brown other sides. Serve immediately. *Preparation time = 45 minutes.*

NUTRITION FACTS—Serving size = 2 pancakes • Servings = 4 • Calories = 189 • Total fat = <1 gm. • Cholesterol (with egg) = 53 mg. • Cholesterol (with egg substitute) = 0 mg. • Sodium = 387 mg. • Total carbohydrate = 35 gm. • Dietary fiber = 3 gm. • Protein = 9 gm.

EXCHANGE VALUES—2 bread/starch

Relaxing Fireside Supper Recipes

CAESAR'S CHICKEN SALAD

4 single skinless chicken breasts (about 4 oz. each)
2 Tbsp. olive oil
1/4 cup orange juice concentrate
1 tsp. Dijon mustard
1/4 tsp. dried thyme
1 tsp. garlic powder
1/4 tsp. red pepper flakes
1/2 head lettuce, chopped
Parmesan cheese (optional)

Cut chicken into thin strips. Sauté in olive oil for 10 to 15 minutes, stirring frequently. Combine orange juice concentrate, mustard, thyme, garlic powder, and pepper flakes, and pour over chicken. Marinate in the refrigerator for at least two hours. Serve on bed of chopped lettuce. Top with Parmesan cheese if desired. *Preparation time = 20 minutes. Marinating time = 2 to 3 hours.*

NUTRITION FACTS—Serving size = 3/4 cup • Servings = 4 • Calories = 258 • Total fat = 11 gm. • Cholesterol = 96 mg. • Sodium = 100 mg. • Total carbohydrate = 2 gm. • Dietary fiber = 0 gm. • Protein = 36 gm.

EXCHANGE VALUES—3 lean meat, 2 fat

MICROWAVE CHEESE POTATOES

6 medium potatoes
4 Tbsp. low-fat margarine
8 oz. nonfat shredded cheddar cheese
8 oz. nonfat sour cream
1/4 tsp. salt
1/2 tsp. white pepper
1/2 cup chopped green onions
Paprika
Nonstick cooking spray

Scrub potatoes and pierce with a fork. Cook in the microwave on high for 20 minutes or until done. Cool slightly; slice the non-peeled potatoes. Set aside. Melt margarine in the microwave. Stir cheese, sour cream, salt, pepper, and onions into the margarine. Stir the cheese mixture into the potatoes. Spray a microwave-safe baking dish with nonstick cooking spray. Spoon the potato mixture into the dish and top with paprika. Cook uncovered on high for 7 to 8 minutes. *Preparation time = 30 minutes.*

NUTRITION FACTS—Serving size = 1/2 cup • Servings = 8 • Calories = 154 • Total fat = 5 gm. • Cholesterol = 10 mg. • Sodium = 299 mg. • Total carbohydrate = 23 gm. • Dietary fiber = 2 gm. • Protein = 7 gm.

EXCHANGE VALUES—1 bread/starch, 1 fat

M.J.'S CHOCOLATE ZUCCHINI POUND CAKE

18-oz. package reduced-fat devils food cake mix
3 eggs (or 3/4 cup egg substitute)
1 1/4 cup buttermilk
1 tsp. cinnamon
6-inch zucchini, washed, and coarsely grated
Nonstick cooking spray

Preheat oven to 375°. In a large mixing bowl, combine cake mix, eggs, buttermilk, and cinnamon. Beat for 3 minutes. Fold in grated zucchini. Pour into 2 loaf pans that have been sprayed with nonstick cooking spray. Bake for 40 to 50 minutes or until the cake tests done. Remove from the oven and cool for 30 minutes before removing from pan. Serve with reduced-fat cherry nut ice milk or raspberry sherbet, if desired. *Preparation time = 30 minutes. Baking time = 50 minutes.*

NUTRITION FACTS—Serving size = 1 piece • Servings = 18 • Calories = 132 • Total fat= 3 gm. • Cholesterol (with real eggs) = 55 mg. • Cholesterol (with egg substitute) = 0 mg. • Total carbohydrate = 26 gm. • Dietary fiber = 1 gm. • Protein = 2 gm. Sodium = 134 mg.

EXCHANGE VALUES—1 1/2 bread/starch

Rainy Day Shopping List

Take this book along to your supermarket or photocopy the list. Select the same number or size of items that you have in the past, based on the number of people for whom you are shopping. Review this list before you go to the store. Cross out items you have on hand, and write in you personal likes and needs.

Produce

Potatoes
Onions
Fruit
Zucchini
Lettuce
Parsley
Green onions

Packaged

Cornmeal
Soup crackers
Coffee
Tea
Reduced fat devils food cake mix
Parmesan cheese

Staples/Spices

Salt
Nutmeg
Dried thyme
Garlic powder
Red pepper flakes
White pepper
Black pepper
Paprika
Cinnamon

Bottled/Canned

Low-salt chicken broth
Syrup
Olive oil
Dijon mustard

Frozen Case

Asparagus
Orange juice

Refrigerated

Skim milk
Nonfat cream cheese
Low-fat margarine
Nonfat cheddar cheese, sharp
Nonfat sour cream
Eggs or egg substitute
Buttermilk

Just for Fun

Meat Case
Chicken breasts

Bakery/Deli
Hard rolls

Other
Nonstick cooking spray

Favorite Sports

Super Sunday

•

Bottom of the Ninth Grand Slam

•

Learning a New Sport

Super Sunday

The sound of cheering echoes throughout the house, strong aromas of tasty fare filter into the room, and family and friends huddle together to witness one of the famous sports events of the year. It's Super Bowl Sunday!

This is a great time to spend with family and close friends, and you don't even have to be a sports fan. Whether you enjoy a small group or a bunch of people, it can be a fun way to share a special Sunday.

In addition to the dishes you prepare, menus can be made even easier by suggesting that others bring their favorite foods or hors d'oeuvres. The more food the better!

SUPER SUNDAY ACTIVITIES

1. Families may want to gather early in the afternoon to prepare food and complete preparation tasks before the pregame show.

2. Prepare hors d'oeuvres to enjoy during the game. Just for fun, design plates that represent your team.

3. Organize a pool of interested adults. Just before the end of the fourth quarter, prepare and dish out a dessert on plates with numbers on the bottoms. Tell everyone not to eat their dessert until the end of the quarter. The person with the winning number gets to eat his or her dessert first.

4. Since the Super Bowl is usually played later in the day, plan on eating your biggest meal before the game starts.

Super Sunday Menus

Cheerleading Breakfast

* Pecan-Stuffed French Toast
   Maple Syrup
   Fruit Spread
* Apple Cups

   Skim Milk
   Grape Juice

Half-Time Huddle

* Stuffed Tomatoes with
   Smoked Turkey and Orzo
* Jicama Salad
   Drinks of Choice

* Oven-Baked Herb
   Potatoes
   Low-Fat Snack Crackers

Football Heroes Smorgasbord

* Italian Meatball Hero Sandwich
* Savory Green Beans
* Peachy Pie

   Skim Milk
   Drinks of Choice

(* recipe follows)

Cheerleading Breakfast Recipes

PECAN-STUFFED FRENCH TOAST

This is a lower fat version of a favorite at the Victorian Swan on Water Bed and Breakfast, Stevens Point, Wisconsin. The original is found in Laura Zahn's Wake Up and Smell the Coffee Cookbook.

> 4 oz. nonfat cream cheese
> 1 tsp. vanilla
> 3 Tbsp. pecans, coarsely chopped
> 2 Tbsp. sugar
> 1 loaf day-old (18-inch) French bread, unsliced
> 3 eggs (or 3/4 cup liquid egg substitute)
> 1/4 cup skim milk
> Cinnamon and/or nutmeg
> Nonstick cooking spray

Blend cream cheese, vanilla, nuts, and 1 tablespoon of sugar together. Slice the bread lengthwise from one end to the other, cutting halfway through the loaf. Be careful not to cut the loaf in two. Spread the cheese mixture evenly along the pocket. Cut the bread in 1 1/2-inch slices. Mix eggs, milk, and the other tablespoon of sugar. Dip the bread into the mixture and let it soak for a few minutes. Cook on a griddle or in a frying pan sprayed with nonstick cooking spray until both sides are golden brown. Sprinkle with cinnamon or nutmeg. Serve with maple syrup or fruit spread. *Preparation time = 30 minutes.*

NUTRITION FACTS—Serving size = 1 1/2-inch slice • Servings = 12 • Calories = 314 • Total fat = 12 gm. • Cholesterol (with egg) = 64 mg. • Cholesterol (with egg substitute) = 10 mg. • Sodium = 502 mg. • Total carbohydrate = 43 mg. • Dietary fiber = 2 gm. • Protein = 9 gm.

EXCHANGE VALUES—3 bread/starch, 1 1/2 fat

APPLE CUPS

2 McIntosh or Delicious apples
Lemon juice
1/2 cup raisins
1/4 cup pecans, chopped
1/4 cup low-fat cream cheese
1/4 cup reduced-fat whipped cream
4 maraschino cherries

Cut apples in half, and remove core. Carefully cut out the center of each half, leaving 1/2 inch to form a cup. Dip each cup in lemon juice to prevent it from getting brown. Add raisins to 1 cup of water and microwave for 3 minutes. Drain. When cool, add pecans, cream cheese, and whipped cream. Spoon mixture into apple cups and garnish with a maraschino cherry. *Preparation time = 15 minutes.*

NUTRITION FACTS—Serving size = 1/2 apple • Servings = 4 • Calories = 234 • Total fat = 13 gm. • Cholesterol = 7 mg. • Sodium = 87 mg. • Total carbohydrate = 31 gm. • Dietary fiber = 1 gm. • Protein = 4 gm.

EXCHANGE VALUES—2 fruit, 2 1/2 fat

Half-Time Huddle Recipes

STUFFED TOMATOES WITH SMOKED TURKEY AND ORZO

8 medium tomatoes
1 1/2 cup orzo, dry
4 cups no-added-salt chicken broth
2 green onions, finely chopped (save tops for garnish)
8 oz. smoked turkey, cut into thin strips
1/8 cup sunflower seeds
2/3 cup low-fat buttermilk ranch dressing

Wash tomatoes. Cut off the top 1/2 inch of each tomato, and scrape out seeds and flesh. (Hint: You can use the tomato seeds and flesh in vegetable soup.) In a medium saucepan, cook orzo in boiling chicken broth until tender, about 12 minutes. Drain well, rinse with cold water, and drain again. In a medium bowl, combine drained orzo with remaining ingredients, stirring to blend. Stuff tomatoes with orzo and turkey mixture. Garnish with finely chopped green onion tops if desired. *Preparation time = 15 minutes. Cooking time = 12 minutes.*

NUTRITION FACTS—Serving size = 1 tomato • Servings = 8 • Calories = 241 • Total fat = 5 gm. • Cholesterol = 23 mg. • Sodium = 106 mg. • Total carbohydrate = 37 gm. • Dietary fiber = 3 gm. • Protein = 12 gm.

EXCHANGE VALUES—2 bread/starch, 1 vegetable, 1 lean meat

OVEN-BAKED HERB POTATOES

2 medium-size baking potatoes
1 Tbsp. canola oil
1/2 tsp. dried thyme
1/2 tsp. dried oregano

Preheat oven to 400°. Scrub potatoes and leave skins on. Slice the potatoes about 1/4-inch thick. Brush the slices with the oil. Place in a baking pan. Sprinkle with the thyme and oregano. Bake for 15 to 20 minutes or until tender. *Preparation time = 15 minutes. Baking time = 20 minutes.*

NUTRITION FACTS—Serving size = 1 cup • Servings = 4 • Calories = 252 • Total fat = 4 gm. • Cholesterol = 0 mg. • Sodium = 16 mg. • Total carbohydrate = 51 gm. • Dietary fiber = <1 gm. • Protein = 5 gm.

EXCHANGE VALUES—2 1/2 bread/starch, 1 fat

JICAMA SALAD

Jicama is a popular Mexican root vegetable that looks like a giant brown turnip. Its crisp white flesh is similar to water chestnuts. Lemon verbena is a spice with a mint-like taste.

> 1 small mango, peeled and cubed
> 1 1/2 cups jicama, cut into julienne strips
>   (about 1 1/2 medium-sized)
> 1 1/2 cups honeydew melon, cut into 1/2-inch cubes
> 2 Tbsp. lime juice
> 2 Tbsp. freshly chopped lemon verbena
> 1 tsp. grated lime peel
> 1 tsp. honey
> 1/4 tsp. salt
> 1/4 cup freshly chopped cilantro

Mix all ingredients in a bowl. Cover and refrigerate for 1 to 2 hours or until chilled. Serve. *Preparation time = 15 minutes. Refrigeration time = 2 hours.*

NUTRITION FACTS—Serving size = 1/2 cup • Servings = 6 • Calories = 49 • Total fat = <1 gm. • Cholesterol = 0 mg. • Sodium = 98 mg. • Total carbohydrate = 13 gm. • Dietary fiber = <1 gm. • Protein = <1 gm.

EXCHANGE VALUES—1 fruit

Football Heroes Smorgasbord Recipes

Italian Meatball Hero Sandwich

1 Tbsp. olive oil
1 small onion, finely chopped
1 clove garlic, crushed
2 tsp. dried oregano
8 oz.-can tomatoes, drained and chopped
1 Tbsp. tomato paste
16-inch loaf French bread (bread crumbs made from center)
2/3 lb. lean ground beef
Salt and pepper to taste
1/3 cup low-fat margarine
6 oz. mozzarella cheese, sliced
Sprigs of fresh watercress to garnish
Nonstick cooking spray
Aluminum foil

To prepare tomato sauce, heat olive oil in a medium-size saucepan. Add onion, garlic, 1 tsp. of oregano, tomatoes, and tomato paste. Cook 10 minutes or until thick, stirring occasionally. Meanwhile, preheat oven to 375°. Slice the bread lengthwise from one end to the other, cutting halfway through the loaf. Do not cut the loaf in two. Remove all the soft bread from the center of both halves, leaving the shell intact. Prepare 2 Tbsp. of bread crumbs from soft bread by chopping fine with a sharp knife.

In a medium-size bowl, combine remaining bread crumbs and ground beef. Season with salt and pepper. Mix well. Form the mixture in 12 small balls. Spray a medium-size skillet with nonstick cooking spray. Heat the skillet, then add meatballs. Fry 5 minutes or until set and golden. Drain on paper towels.

Spread inside of bread shell with 3 Tbsp. of margarine and add half the tomato sauce. Fill bread shell with meatballs and spoon sauce over meatballs. Cover with half the cheese slices. Press bread shell together. Spread the remaining margarine on the outside of the shell and cover with remaining slices of cheese and oregano. Completely wrap the sandwich in greased foil. Bake for 20 minutes. Unwrap the foil to expose the sandwich, and bake 8 to 10 minutes more or until crisp. Cut in 4 thick pieces. Garnish with watercress. *Preparation time = 30 minutes. Cooking time = 30 minutes.*

NUTRITION FACTS—Serving size = 4-inch slice • Servings = 4 • Calories = 420 • Total fat = 10 gm. • Cholesterol = 41 mg. • Sodium = 772 mg. • Total carbohydrate = 56 gm. • Dietary fiber = 3 gm. • Protein = 25 gm.

EXCHANGE VALUES—2 1/2 bread/starch, 2 lean meat, 2 fat

SAVORY GREEN BEANS

1 lb. fresh green beans (about 4 cups)
1 cup water
1/2 cup onion, chopped
10 3/4-oz. can Healthy Request® low-fat cream of mushroom soup
1/4 cup skim milk
1 tsp. savory
1/2 cup nonfat grated cheddar cheese
Nonstick cooking spray

Preheat oven to 350°. Cook beans in water in covered saucepan for 15 minutes. Drain. Add onion, mushrooms, soup, milk, and savory. Heat until well blended. Spray casserole dish with nonstick cooking spray. Place the mixture into the casserole dish, and sprinkle cheese on top. Bake covered for 15 minutes and uncovered for 15 minutes. *Preparation time = 15 minutes. Baking time = 30 minutes.*

NUTRITION FACTS—Serving size = 3/4 cup • Servings = 8 • Calories = 61 • Total fat = 1 gm. • Cholesterol = 4 mg. • Sodium = 219 mg. • Total carbohydrate = 9 gm. • Dietary fiber = 2 gm. • Protein = 5 gm.

EXCHANGE VALUES—1/2 bread/starch, 1 vegetable

PEACHY PIE

9-inch unbaked pie shell
5 cups fresh peaches, sliced
1 cup sugar
1/3 cup low-fat margarine
1/3 cup flour
1 beaten egg (or 1/4 cup egg substitute)
1/2 tsp. vanilla
1/4 cup brown sugar
1/2 cup flour
1/4 cup low-fat margarine

Preheat oven to 350°. Place peaches level full in unbaked pie shell. Set aside. Cream together sugar and 1/3 cup margarine. Add flour, egg, and vanilla. Mix and spread over peaches. Mix together brown sugar, flour, and 1/4 cup margarine. Crumble over top of pie. Bake for 1 hour. *Preparation time = 30 minutes. Baking time = 1 hour.*

NUTRITION FACTS—Serving size = 1 piece • Servings = 8 • Calories = 377 • Total fat = 13 gm. • Cholesterol (with egg) = 27 mg. • Cholesterol (with egg substitute) = 0 mg. • Sodium = 226 mg. • Total carbohydrate = 65 gm. • Dietary fiber = 3 gm. • Protein = 4 gm.

EXCHANGE VALUES—3 bread/starch, 1 fruit, 2 fat

NOTE: THIS RECIPE MAY NOT BE SUITABLE FOR INDIVIDUALS FOLLOWING A DIET LOW IN SIMPLE SUGARS OR CONTROLLED FOR TRIGLYCERIDES.

Super Sunday Shopping List

Take this book along to your supermarket or photocopy the list. Select the same number or size of items that you have in the past, based on the number of people for whom you are shopping. Review this list before you go to the store. Cross out items you have on hand, and write in your personal likes and needs.

Produce

Green onions
Onions
Peaches
Apples
Potatoes
Green beans
Garlic
Watercress
Tomatoes
Mango
Jicama
Honeydew melon
Cilantro
Lime

Staples/Spices

Nutmeg
Salt
Pepper
Flour
Vanilla
Sugar
Brown sugar
Thyme
Oregano
Savory
Olive oil
Cinnamon
Lemon verbena

Packaged

Raisins
Pecans
Nonfat Parmesan cheese
Sunflower seeds
Orzo
Coffee
Tea

Bottled/Canned

No-added-salt chicken broth
Low-fat buttermilk ranch dressing
Mushrooms
Healthy Request® low fat cream of mushroom soup
Grape juice
Honey
Tomato paste
Maraschino cherries

Favorite Sports

Frozen Case

9-inch unbaked pie shell
Reduced-fat whipped topping

Refrigerator Case

Low-fat margarine
Eggs or egg substitute
Low-fat cream cheese
Skim milk
Nonfat cheddar cheese
Nonfat cream cheese
Nonfat mozzarella cheese

Meat Case

Lean ground beef
Smoked turkey

Bakery/Deli

18-inch unsliced loaf day-old
    French bread
16-inch loaf French bread

Snack Foods

Low-fat snack crackers

Other

Nonstick cooking spray
Aluminum foil

Bottom of the Ninth Grand Slam

It's the last game of the season. The two best junior league teams are playing for the championship. The score at the bottom of the ninth inning is Cardinals—5, Smokey Bears—4. The Smokey Bears are up to bat...

Baseball is a sport everyone can enjoy as either a player or a spectator.

Some of the values we learn in baseball can be related to family and mealtime. Just as a player who goes to bat needs to be well prepared, so does the person making dinner; it can make all the difference.

Bottom of the Ninth Grand Slam Activities

1. As you set up the roster for foods that are up to bat, rotating batters, or the foods you eat, makes mealtime more enjoyable.

2. When shopping for food, teach your children to check labels for nutrition values. Teach them what to look for in fresh produce and meat, fish, and chicken.

3. Wash fruits and vegetables to avoid food bacteria. Also, cook meat to the right internal temperature.

Bottom of the Ninth Grand Slam Menus

All Day Baseball Lunch

* Hamburger Bean Cookout
* Cucumber Spice
* Twice-Baked Squash

Whole Wheat Bread
Soft Drinks

Second Inning Baseball Dinner

* Carrot Soup
* Tossed Garden Salad

* Baking Powder Biscuits
Skim Milk

World Series Supper

* Mushroom Turkey Casserole
* Garlic Beans
* Sassy Applesauce With Dumplings

Skim Milk
Coffee or Tea

(* recipe follows)

All Day Baseball Lunch Recipes

HAMBURGER BEAN COOKOUT

1 lb. 93% fat-free ground beef
1 medium onion, diced
1/2 cup celery, diced
15 1/2-oz. can pork and beans, undrained
15 1/2-oz. can red kidney beans, drained
15 1/2-oz. can butter beans, drained
1/2 cup brown sugar
1/8 cup molasses
1 Tbsp. prepared mustard
8-oz. can no-salt tomato sauce
1 Tbsp. liquid smoke

Brown ground beef, onion, and celery. Drain well. Add the rest of the ingredients. Mixture can be put in a Crockpot on low heat for 3 to 4 hours or placed in a saucepan on low heat for an hour. Either way, stir several times during the slow-cooking process. *Preparation time = 15 minutes. Crockpot cooking time = 3 to 4 hours. Stovetop cooking time = 1 hour.*

NUTRITION FACTS—Serving size = 3/4 cup • Servings = 8 • Calories = 374 • Total fat = 10 gm. • Cholesterol = 53 mg. • Sodium = 395 mg. • Total carbohydrate = 48 gm. • Dietary fiber = 6 gm. • Protein = 26 gm.

EXCHANGE VALUES—2 1/2 bread/starch, 3 lean meat, 1/2 fat

CUCUMBER SPICE

3 medium cucumbers
1 small onion, sliced thin
2 cups water
1/2 tsp. salt
1/2 cup cider vinegar
1/2 cup sugar
1/8 tsp. white pepper
1/2 tsp. celery seed

Peel cucumbers and slice about 1/4-inch thick. Add onion, water, and salt. Mix well. Let stand 15 minutes. Drain cucumber mixture in colander. Heat vinegar, sugar, pepper, and celery seed in microwave on high for 2 to 3 minutes, stirring once. Pour over cucumber mixture. Refrigerate for at least an hour before serving. *Preparation time = 20 minutes. Refrigeration time = 1 hour.*

NUTRITION FACTS—Serving size = 1/2 cup • Servings = 8 • Calories = 70 • Total fat = <1 gm. • Cholesterol 0 mg. • Sodium = 136 mg. • Total carbohydrate = 17 gm. • Dietary fiber = <1 gm. • Protein = <1 gm.

EXCHANGE VALUES—2 vegetable

TWICE-BAKED SQUASH

3 acorn squash, cut into 6 halves (seeds removed)
1 cup water
2 cups frozen chopped broccoli
2 medium-size carrots, thinly sliced
1 tsp. Italian herb seasoning
1 tsp. garlic powder
1/2 tsp. nutmeg
1/4 tsp. white pepper
10 3/4-oz. can Healthy Request® low-fat cream of broccoli soup
8 oz. nonfat mozzarella cheese, grated

Preheat oven to 375°. Bake squash for 45 minutes or microwave covered squash on high for 15 to 25 minutes, or until rind is easy to cut through. Set aside. Boil broccoli and carrots in water for 8 to 10 minutes. Drain. Set aside. Combine remaining ingredients, except mozzarella cheese, and add to broccoli and carrot mixture. Reheat for 5 to 7 minutes, stirring occasionally. Spoon over squash, adding about 2 Tbsp. grated cheese to each squash half. Reheat in the oven for 8 to 10 minutes, until cheese is melted. *Preparation time = 15 minutes. Baking time = 1 hour.*

NUTRITION FACTS—Serving size = 1/2 squash • Servings = 6 • Calories = 222 • Total fat = 2 gm. • Cholesterol = 3 mg. • Sodium = 366 mg. • Total carbohydrate = 47 gm. • Dietary fiber = 0 gm. • Protein = 11 gm.

EXCHANGE VALUES—2 bread/starch, 1 vegetable, 1/2 skim milk

Second Inning Baseball Dinner Recipes

CARROT SOUP

1 lb. carrots
1 small onion
1 medium-size potato
2 Tbsp. low-fat margarine
3 cups clear vegetable broth
Pinch of sugar
2/3 cup skim milk
1 tsp. white pepper
2 Tbsp. flour
1/2 tsp. salt

OPTIONAL:

2 tsp. fresh parsley
1/2 cup croutons
1/2 cup nonfat sour cream

Peel and chunk carrots. Place in blender. Process mixture to a puree. Empty into a 1 1/2 quart saucepan. Peel and chop onion. Puree in blender. (It's not necessary to rinse the blender between vegetables.) Add pureed onions to mixture in saucepan. Peel and dice potato. Puree in blender. Add to mixture in saucepan. Add margarine to saucepan mixture. Cook 2 minutes on medium heat. Add vegetable broth and sugar. Cook on medium heat for 30 minutes. Reduce heat to simmer. Combine skim milk, white pepper, flour, and salt in a gravy toddy. (Hint: Any tight-lidded jar can function as an old-fashioned toddy shaker.) Shake well for a minute. Add mixture to saucepan, stirring slowly. Cook on low heat for 5 minutes or until thickened. If desired, sprinkle with parsley, and serve with croutons and a dollop of sour cream. *Preparation time = 30 minutes. Cooking time = 40 minutes.*

NUTRITION FACTS—Serving size = 1 cup • Servings = 6 • Calories = 106 • Total fat = 2 gm. • Cholesterol <1 mg. • Sodium 571 mg. • Total carbohydrate = 17 gm. • Dietary fiber = 3 gm. • Protein = 5 gm.

EXCHANGE VALUES—1 bread/starch, 1 vegetable

TOSSED GARDEN SALAD

1 cup fresh spinach, shredded
1 cup lettuce, shredded
1 cup endive, shredded
1/4 cup diced celery
6 radishes, sliced
1/4 cup sliced onion
1 cup low-fat French dressing

Put all vegetables in a salad bowl and toss. Refrigerate. Just before serving, add dressing. Toss lightly until well mixed. *Preparation time = 15 minutes. Refrigeration time = 30 minutes (optional).*

NUTRITION FACTS—Serving size = 1 cup • Servings = 4 • Calories = 104 • Total fat = 4 gm. • Cholesterol = 4 mg. • Sodium = 510 mg. • Total carbohydrate = 17 gm. • Dietary fiber = 1 gm. • Protein = 2 gm.

EXCHANGE VALUES—2 vegetable, 1 fat

BAKING POWDER BISCUITS

2 cups flour
1 Tbsp. baking powder
1/2 tsp. salt
1/3 cup low-fat margarine
3/4 cup skim milk

Preheat oven to 450°. In a mixing bowl, thoroughly stir together flour, baking powder, and salt. Add margarine and cut in until mixture resembles coarse crumbs. Make a well in the dry mixture and add the milk all at once. Stir just until dough clings together. On a lightly floured surface, knead dough gently for 10 to 12 strokes. Roll dough to 1/2-inch thickness. Cut with a 2 1/2-inch biscuit cutter, dipping cutter in flour between cuts. Transfer biscuits to an ungreased baking sheet. Bake for 10 to 12 minutes or until golden brown. Serve immediately. *Preparation time = 15 minutes. Baking time = 12 minutes.*

NUTRITION FACTS—Serving size = 1 biscuit • Servings = 12 • Calories = 103 • Total fat = 3 gm. • Cholesterol = <1 mg. • Sodium = 261 mg. • Total carbohydrate = 17 gm. • Dietary fiber = <1 gm. • Protein = 3 gm.

EXCHANGE VALUES—1 bread/starch, 1/2 fat

World Series Supper Recipes

MUSHROOM TURKEY CASSEROLE

6 oz. broad noodles
7 oz. lean turkey, shaved
1/2 cup celery, chopped
2 Tbsp. chopped fresh green pepper
4 oz. fresh mushrooms, sliced
1 Tbsp. olive oil
10 1/2-oz. can low-fat cream of mushroom soup
10 1/2-oz. can low-fat cream of chicken soup
2/3 cup skim milk
Nonstick cooking spray
4 oz. nonfat cheddar cheese

Preheat oven to 375°. Cook noodles according to package directions. Drain and set aside. Sauté turkey, celery, green pepper, and mushrooms in olive oil for 5 to 10 minutes. Add soup, milk, and noodles to vegetables. Place in casserole sprayed with nonstick cooking spray. Top with cheese. Cook in oven or microwave for 10 minutes. *Preparation time = 20 minutes. Baking time = 10 minutes.*

NUTRITION FACTS—Serving size = 1 cup • Servings = 10 • Calories = 103 • Total fat = 3 gm. • Cholesterol = <1 mg. • Sodium = 261 mg. • Total carbohydrate = 17 gm. • Dietary fiber = <1 gm. • Protein = 3 gm.

EXCHANGE VALUES—1 bread/starch, 1/2 fat

GARLIC BEANS

1 lb. fresh green beans
1/2 cup water
1 Tbsp. low-fat margarine
1 Tbsp. lemon juice
1 tsp. chopped garlic
1/4 cup wine vinegar
1 tsp. sugar

Boil beans in water until tender. Drain. Add remaining ingredients. Rewarm for one minute in microwave, if necessary. This is very zesty. *Preparation time = 15 minutes.*

NUTRITION FACTS—Serving size = 1/2 cup • Servings = 4 • Calories = 38 • Total fat = 2 gm. • Cholesterol = 0 mg. • Sodium = 34 mg. • Total carbohydrate = 7 gm. • Dietary fiber = 0 • Protein = <1 gm.

EXCHANGE VALUES—1 vegetable

SASSY APPLESAUCE WITH DUMPLINGS

APPLESAUCE:

4 cups cooking apples, pared and sliced
1 cup water
2 Tbsp. orange juice concentrate
1 tsp. cinnamon
1/2 tsp. cardamom
1/2 tsp. allspice
2 Tbsp. brown sugar

DUMPLINGS:

1 cup reduced-fat Bisquick
2/3 cup skim milk
1 Tbsp. brown sugar
1/2 tsp. cinnamon

Place all applesauce ingredients in saucepan. Cook for about 15 minutes, or until apples are soft but not mushy. To make dumplings, mix all dumpling ingredients together. Drop tablespoon-sized amounts of dough on the applesauce and cook, uncovered, for 5 minutes. Cover and cook 5 minutes more. *Preparation time = 15 minutes. Cooking time = 25 minutes.*

NUTRITION FACTS—Serving Size = 3/4 cup • Servings = 4 • Calories = 294 • Total fat = 3 gm. • Cholesterol = <1 mg. • Sodium = 378 mg. • Total carbohydrate = 68 gm. • Dietary fiber = 5 gm. • Protein = 4 gm.

EXCHANGE VALUES—2 bread/starch, 2 fruit, 1/2 fat

Bottom of the Ninth Grand Slam Shopping List

Take this book along to your supermarket or photocopy the list. Select the same number or size of items as you have in the past, based on the number of people for whom you are shopping. Review this list before you go to the store. Cross out items you have on hand, and write in your personal likes and needs.

Produce

Celery
Carrots
Onions
Potatoes
Fresh parsley
Garlic
Apples
Tomato
Cucumbers
Acorn squash
Spinach
Cilantro
Lettuce
Endive
Mushrooms
Green pepper
Green beans
Radishes

Packaged

Italian herb seasoning
Croutons
Reduced-fat Bisquick
Broad noodles
Coffee
Tea

Staples/Spices

Garlic powder
Nutmeg
Brown sugar
Sugar
Flour
Salt
Celery seed
Cinnamon
Cardamom
Allspice
Baking powder
White pepper

Bottled/Canned

Olive oil
Wine vinegar

The Quality Time Family Cookbook

Low-fat French dressing
Low-fat cream
 of broccoli soup
Low-fat cream
 of mushroom soup
Low-fat cream
 of chicken soup
Molasses
Liquid smoke
Clear vegetable broth
Pork and beans
Kidney beans
Butter beans
Prepared mustard
No-salt tomato sauce

Frozen Case

Orange juice
Chopped broccoli

Refrigerator Case

Low-fat margarine
Skim milk
Nonfat sour cream
Nonfat mozzarella cheese
Nonfat cheddar cheese

Meat Case

Extra lean ground beef
Lean turkey, shaved

Bakery/Deli

Whole wheat bread

Other

Nonstick cooking spray
Soft drinks

LEARNING A NEW SPORT

What a perfect day to play—the family is running around outside, enjoying outdoor activities together. "Throw the ball here," your daughter yells. Everyone is having so much fun!

One way to initiate quality family time is to identify activities the whole family can enjoy. There are a lot of exciting things to do out there, but usually someone in my family wants to try something new.

You may want to set a goal to learn a new sport or leisure activity every year. This is a way for everyone to improve their skills and for families to share time together.

LEARNING NEW SPORT ACTIVITIES

1. Brainstorm about sports and leisure activities your family may be interested in learning or improving. Make a list and refer back to it when you need to.

2. From the list, determine which activities family members want to learn first; then write down the ones that will be fun for the entire family. Here are some suggestions:

Archery	Fishing
Boating	Gardening
Backpacking	Horseshoes
Biking	Jogging
Bird-watching	Kite flying
Canoeing	Sailing
Dancing	Walking

3. Set a family goal and a tentative completion date. This may help motivate your family to meet that goal.

Learning a New Sport Menus

What's the Plan Supper

* Cornish Hens with Raspberry Chutney
* Parsley Potatoes
* Moist Heath-Bit Cookies
  Whole Wheat Bread
* Banana Pepper and Cucumber Salad
  Coffee or Tea
  Skim Milk

Read the Rules Breakfast

* Toasted Raisin-Wheat Bread
  Fruit Spread
  Orange Juice
  Skim Milk

Aching Muscles Lunch

* Baked Potato Melts
  Spinach Salad
* Strawberry Jello Dessert
  Skim Milk
  Coffee or Tea

What's the Plan Supper Recipes

CORNISH HENS WITH RASPBERRY CHUTNEY

2 Cornish hens, cut in half
16-oz. can reduced-sugar peach slices, drained (reserve syrup)
1 Tbsp. cornstarch
1 cup fresh or frozen red raspberries
1 cup peeled, chopped apple
1/4 cup wine vinegar
1 Tbsp. onion, chopped
1/4 cup brown sugar, firmly packed
1 tsp. cinnamon
1/2 tsp. ginger
1/2 tsp. nutmeg
Nonstick cooking spray
Spinach leaves or cilantro for garnish

Preheat oven to 350°. Spray a small baking dish with nonstick cooking spray. Place Cornish hens in baking dish and roast for 45 minutes. To make chutney, mix reserved peach syrup with cornstarch. Set aside. Combine peach slices with remaining ingredients and heat thoroughly. When mixture begins to bubble, add peach syrup slowly, while continuing to stir until mixture thickens. When hens are done, place on a serving platter and pour chutney over hens. Garnish with spinach leaves or cilantro. Serve any extra chutney in a small dish on the platter. *Preparation time = 15 minutes. Baking time = 45 minutes.*

NUTRITION FACTS—Serving size = 1/2 hen • Servings = 4 • Calories = 333 • Total fat = 12 gm. • Cholesterol = 85 mg. • Sodium = 55 mg. • Total carbohydrate = 29 gm. • Dietary fiber = <1 gm. • Protein = 30 gm.

EXCHANGE VALUES—3 lean meat, 2 bread/starch, 1/2 fat

PARSLEY POTATOES

11 or 12 medium-sized red potatoes
3 Tbsp. low-fat margarine, melted
1 Tbsp. parsley flakes

Boil potatoes whole until fork penetrates easily to center of potato. Cut potatoes in half. Drizzle melted margarine over potatoes; sprinkle with parsley flakes. *Preparation time = 20 minutes.*

NUTRITION FACTS—Serving size = 3/4 cup • Servings = 8 • Calories = 171 • Total fat = 3 gm. • Cholesterol = 0 mg. • Sodium = 49 mg. • Total carbohydrate = 30 gm. • Dietary fiber = 2 gm. • Protein = 4 gm.

EXCHANGE VALUES—2 bread/starch, 1/2 fat

BANANA PEPPER AND CUCUMBER SALAD

1 medium banana pepper, finely diced
1 medium white onion, cut into thin wedges
4 medium cucumbers, peeled and sliced thin
1 1/2 tsp. salt
6 ice cubes
3 Tbsp. vinegar
2 Tbsp. sugar
1/2 tsp. celery seed

In a large bowl, mix diced pepper, onion wedges, cucumber slices, salt, and ice cubes. Cover and refrigerate for at least 2 hours, stirring twice. Drain vegetables in a colander, then press liquid from vegetables with a paper towel. Return vegetables to a serving bowl. Sprinkle with vinegar, sugar, and celery seed. Stir for 2 minutes to dissolve sugar, then serve. *Preparation time = 15 minutes. Refrigeration time = 2 hours.*

NUTRITION FACTS—Serving size = 1 cup • Servings = 8 • Calories = 19 • Total fat = 0 gm. • Cholesterol = 0 mg. • Sodium = 201 mg. • Total carbohydrate = 5 gm. • Dietary fiber = <1 gm. • Protein = 1 gm.

EXCHANGE VALUES—1 vegetable

MOIST HEATH-BIT COOKIES

1/2 cup low-fat margarine
1/2 cup brown sugar, firmly packed
1 egg (or 1/4 cup liquid egg substitute)
1 tsp. vanilla
1 cup applesauce, no sugar added
2 1/2 cups flour
1 tsp. baking soda
1 package (6 oz.) Heath Bits
Nonstick cooking spray

Preheat oven to 350°. Spray cookie sheet with nonstick cooking spray. Cream margarine and brown sugar. Add egg and vanilla. Add half the applesauce and half of the dry ingredients, and blend thoroughly. Add remaining half. Fold in Heath Bits. Drop by teaspoonfuls onto cookie sheet and bake for 10 minutes. *Preparation time = 15 minutes. Baking time = 10 minutes.*

NUTRITION FACTS—Serving size = 1 cookie • Servings = 42 • Calories = 138 • Total fat = 1 gm. • Cholesterol (with egg) = 5 mg. • Cholesterol (with egg substitute) = <1 mg. • Sodium = 60 mg. • Total carbohydrate = 32 gm. • Dietary fiber = <1 gm. • Protein = <1 gm.

EXCHANGE VALUES—1 bread/starch, 1 fruit

Read the Rules Breakfast Recipes

RAISIN WHEAT BREAD

2 packages dry yeast
1 Tbsp. sugar
1 cup warm water
1 cup raisins
1 cup water
1/3 cup honey
3 Tbsp. low-fat margarine
1 tsp. salt
2 cups whole wheat flour
4 1/2 cups white flour
Nonstick cooking spray

Preheat oven to 375°. Spray two loaf pans with nonstick cooking spray. Add yeast and sugar to 1 cup warm water. Let stand 15 minutes. Microwave raisins in 1 cup water for 3 minutes; drain. In a large bowl, combine yeast mixture, honey, margarine, salt, and drained raisins. Gradually add flour until mixture reaches kneading consistency. (You may need another 1/4 cup flour so dough can be handled.) Knead for about 5 minutes, then place in a bowl sprayed with nonstick cooking spray. Rub top of dough with margarine. Let rise until double, then knead again. When dough has doubled again, divide into two even pieces. Knead again, flatten, then roll up tight to the size of the pan. Place in loaf pans. Rub tops of loaves lightly with margarine. Let rise until double. Bake 40 to 45 minutes. Remove loaves from pans, and cool on racks. *Preparation time = 2 hours. Baking time = 45 minutes.*

NUTRITION FACTS—Serving size = 1/15 of loaf • Servings = 30 • Calories = 150 • Total fat = 3 gm. • Cholesterol = 0 mg. • Sodium = 83 mg. • Total carbohydrate = 28 gm. • Dietary fiber = 2 gm. • Protein = 3 gm.

EXCHANGE VALUES—1 1/2 bread/starch, 1/2 fat

Aching Muscles Lunch Recipes

BAKED POTATO MELTS

4 baking potatoes
2 chicken breasts
1 Tbsp. olive oil
2 cups broccoli
1 cup nonfat grated cheddar cheese
4 cherry tomatoes (for garnish)

Preheat oven to 400°. Bake potatoes for 45 minutes. While potatoes are baking, cube, and brown chicken breasts in skillet in olive oil. Set aside. Steam broccoli in saucepan or in microwave. Drain before using. Build potato melts by slicing a pocket in each potato. Using a pot holder, squeeze the potato open. Spoon cubed chicken breast and steamed broccoli in layers over the opened potato; top with grated cheddar cheese. Serve with a cherry tomato as a garnish. *Preparation time = 10 minutes. Baking time = 45 minutes.*

NUTRITION FACTS—Serving size = 1 potato and 1/2 cup sauce • Servings = 4 • Calories = 467 • Total fat = 7 gm. • Cholesterol = 73 mg. • Sodium = 303 mg. • Total carbohydrate = 59 gm. • Dietary fiber = 4 gm. • Protein = 43 gm.

EXCHANGE VALUES—3 lean meat, 4 bread/starch

STRAWBERRY JELLO DESSERT

1 lg. package sugar-free strawberry-banana Jello
2 cups vanilla yogurt
1 cup fresh or frozen strawberries, no sugar added
1 banana
Reduced-fat whipped topping

Prepare Jello according to package directions. Refrigerate until thickened, then beat with a mixer until fluffy. Fold in yogurt and strawberries. Pour mixture into serving dishes. Refrigerate until completely set. Before serving, frost top with whipped topping, and garnish with sliced banana. *Preparation time = 15 minutes. Refrigeration time = 1 hour.*

NUTRITION FACTS—Serving size = 1/2 cup • Servings = 6 • Calories = 86 • Total fat = <1 gm. • Cholesterol = 4 mg. • Sodium = 67 mg. • Total carbohydrate = 13 gm. • Dietary fiber = <1 gm. • Protein = 6 gm.

EXCHANGE VALUES—1 bread/starch

THINGS TO GET DONE

TRASH OR TREASURE
•
BACK TO SCHOOL
•
COUNTY FAIR
•
HOLIDAY SHOPPING

Trash or Treasure

Everyone rose at dawn to arrange tables and baked goods for the sale. Old favorites cover the patio picnic table. The wooden barn and croquet set that were special to Mom and Dad now sit on a shelf waiting for an interested buyer. Today's tag sale day!

It may be difficult to sell some items from your past, but getting rid of some clutter can help you become more organized. Planning ahead will give you the time you need to make good decisions about what you want to sell or keep.

Everyone appreciates quick meals when you're working on a tag sale. The menu suggestions in this section are delicious and easy. Have fun watching your clutter turn into cash!

Trash or Treasure Activities

1. Plan the sale three or four months before the tentative date; clear all schedules. You may want to invite several neighborhood families to join you.

2. Ask each family member to select garage sale items at least two weeks before the date.

3. Clean all items and get them into prime condition. Price items using various colored stick-on dots to track each person's sales. Store marked items in bags or boxes.

4. Decide if you will sell beverages or baked goods. Selling baked goods is a great way to boost overall sales. Don't forget coffee; the aroma of freshly brewed coffee can draw in people who are just passing by. And you may want to sell ice-cold pop if it's a hot day.

5. Determine how much display area you will need. Find plenty of tables and shelves.

6. Make sure you have plenty of change on hand. You'll need about $25 to $50 worth of small bills and coins.
7. Consider saving the profit and applying it to a family getaway weekend or a community project in need of financial support. This is a good way to help your children learn the rewards of sharing blessings with others.
8. Consider asking a not-for-profit organization to pick up useful items that do not sell. Get a signed receipt so you can deduct the donation on your taxes.

Trash or Treasure Menus

Night Before Madness Supper

* Hot Submarine Sandwiches
* Marinated Muskmelon
   Skim Milk

Breakfast at Dawn

* Orange Oatmeal Muffins	Orange Juice
* Crockpot Fruit Soup	Coffee or Tea

Tag Sale Day Lunch

* Meatless Vegetable Stew	Skim Milk
Tossed Salad	Coffee or Tea
Choice of Dressing	Chocolate Pudding Pops

(* recipe follows)

Night Before Madness Supper Recipes

HOT SUBMARINE SANDWICHES

*4 loaves hard-crust French bread
(each about 8-inches long)
1/2 cup nonfat mayonnaise
1/4 cup fresh ground basil
2 cloves garlic, crushed
2 cups shredded lettuce
1 cup finely sliced red onions
1 cup sliced green bell peppers
12 slices tomato
8 oz. sliced skinless turkey breast
8 oz. thinly sliced mozzarella
Aluminum foil*

Preheat oven to 400°. Slice French bread loaves lengthwise without cutting all the way through them. Combine mayonnaise, basil, and garlic. Spread mixture on the inside of each loaf. Arrange lettuce, onions, peppers, and tomatoes on the bread. Top with turkey, and finish with a layer of cheese. Wrap tightly in aluminum foil. Heat sandwiches in the oven for 10 to 15 minutes or until warmed through. Cut each sandwich in half, and serve at once. *Preparation time = 15 minutes. Baking time = 15 minutes.*

NUTRITION FACTS—Serving size = 4" slice • Servings = 8 • Calories = 420 • Total fat = 10 gm. • Cholesterol = 24 mg. • Sodium = 1,024 mg. • Total carbohydrate = 65 gm. • Dietary fiber = 5 gm. • Protein = 23 gm.

EXCHANGE VALUES—3 bread/starch, 1 skim milk, 2 fat

MARINATED MUSKMELON

This fragrant fruit dish was developed by M.J. Smith, one of my dearest friends and mentors.

>*1 large muskmelon (Check for ripeness by smelling the melon; it should be fragrant.)*
>*1 cup apricot nectar*
>*2 tsp. finely grated lime peeling*

Peel melon, slice, and cut into 1-inch chunks. Place melon chunks in a large bowl, pour nectar over melon, and stir in lime peeling. Refrigerate for at least an hour. Use a ladle or slotted spoon to serve melon into fruit bowls. *Preparation time = 10 minutes. Refrigeration time = 1 hour.*

NUTRITION FACTS—Serving size = 1 cup • Servings = 6 • Calories = 55 • Total fat = 0 gm. • Cholesterol = 0 mg. • Sodium = 9 mg. • Total carbohydrate = 13 gm. • Dietary fiber = 1 gm. • Protein = 1 gm.

EXCHANGE VALUES—1 fruit

Breakfast at Dawn Recipes

ORANGE OATMEAL MUFFINS

Nonstick cooking spray
1 orange
1 1/4 cup flour
1 cup oatmeal
1/3 cup brown sugar
1/2 tsp. baking powder
1/2 tsp. baking soda
1/4 tsp. salt
1/3 cup low-fat margarine
1 apple, peeled and chopped
2 eggs (or 1/2 cup liquid egg substitute)
1/2 cup buttermilk

Preheat oven to 400°. Spray muffin tins with nonstick cooking spray. Finely shred 1 tsp. of peel from the orange. Squeeze 1/2 cup of juice. Set aside. Mix flour, oatmeal, brown sugar, baking powder, and salt. Cut in low-fat margarine until mixture resembles coarse meal. Mix in apples. Beat together eggs, orange peel, orange juice, and buttermilk; add all at once to dry mixture. Stir lightly to dampen dry ingredients. Fill muffin cups about 3/4 full. Bake 15 to 20 minutes. *Preparation time = 15 minutes. Baking time = 20 minutes.*

NUTRITION FACTS—Serving size = 1 muffin • Servings = 12 • Calories = 113 • Total fat = 2 gm. • Cholesterol (with egg) = 36 mg. • Cholesterol (with egg substitute) = <1 mg. • Sodium = 213 mg. • Total carbohydrate = 21 gm. • Dietary fiber = <1 gm. • Protein = 3 gm.

EXCHANGE VALUES—1 bread/starch, 1/2 fat

CROCKPOT FRUIT SOUP

Decorah, Iowa, is "the little Norway" of the Midwest. Irma Johnson is a native and recommended this versatile Norwegian recipe.

> *3/4 cup pearl tapioca*
> *1 qt. water*
> *1 lb. raisins*
> *1/2 lb. dried apricots*
> *1 lb. pitted prunes*
> *1 cup sugar*
> *1 qt. grape juice*
> *1 can pitted Bing cherries*
> *1/4 tsp. salt*
> *Juice of 1 lemon*
> *2 sticks cinnamon*

Cook pearl tapioca with water on low for several hours until tapioca becomes transparent. Add all remaining ingredients. Serve either hot or cold. For a lighter syrup, use orange juice instead of grape juice, white raisins instead of dark, fruit cocktail instead of pitted prunes, and red sour cherries instead of Bing. These changes will help you adjust the sweetness. Almost any type of leftover fruit can be added; wine can also be added. Serve cold or warm. *Cooking time = 1 to 3 hours.*

NUTRITION FACTS—Serving size = 1/2 cup • Servings = 20 • Calories = 216 • Total fat = <1 gm. • Cholesterol = 0 mg. • Sodium = 32 mg. • Total carbohydrate = 56 gm. • Dietary fiber = 2 gm. • Protein = 2 gm.

EXCHANGE VALUES—1 bread/starch, 2 fruit

Tag Sale Day Lunch Recipes

MEATLESS VEGETABLE STEW

1 qt. cubed turnips
4 to 5 carrots, scrubbed and sliced
5 kale leaves, coarsely chopped
1 cup coarsely chopped onion
1 Tbsp. low-fat margarine
1 Tbsp. flour
1/4 tsp. salt
1 tsp. curry powder
1 cup cold skim milk

Cook turnips, carrots, kale, and onion in a 1-quart saucepan over medium heat for 10 minutes, then simmer for 20 minutes. Set aside. Melt margarine in microwave. Stir in flour, salt, and curry powder until smooth. Stir in cold milk gradually, and cook over medium heat, stirring constantly until sauce boils and becomes thick and smooth. Add white sauce to cooked vegetables in their juice. *Preparation time = 15 minutes. Cooking time = 30 minutes.*

NUTRITION FACTS—Serving size = 1 cup • Servings = 5 • Calories = 114 • Total fat = 2 gm. • Cholesterol = 1 mg. • Sodium = 277 mg. • Total carbohydrate = 22 gm. • Dietary fiber = 3 gm. • Protein = 5 gm.

EXCHANGE VALUES—1 bread/starch, 1 vegetable

Trash or Treasure Shopping List

Take this book along to your supermarket or photocopy the list. Select the same number or size of items that you have in the past, based on the number of people for whom you are shopping. Review this list before you go to the store. Cross out items you have on hand, and write in your personal likes and needs.

Produce

Turnips
Apples
Lettuce
Onions
Red onions
Green bell peppers
Tomatoes
Lemon
Lime
Carrots
Kale
Muskmelon
Orange
Garlic cloves
Basil, fresh ground

Packaged

Dried apricots
Pitted prunes
Oatmeal
Tapioca, pearl
Raisins
Coffee/Tea

Staples

Flour
Brown sugar
Baking powder
Baking soda
Salt
Sugar
Cinnamon sticks
Curry powder

Bottled/Canned

Choice of dressing
Apricot nectar
Grape juice
Bing cherries

Frozen Case

Orange juice
Chocolate pudding pops

Refrigerator Case

Nonfat mayonnaise
Mozzarella cheese
Low-fat margarine
Skim milk
Buttermilk
Eggs or egg substitute

Meat Case

Skinless turkey breast

Bakery/Deli

Hard-crust French bread
   (each loaf 8-inches long)

Other

Aluminum foil
Nonstick cooking spray

Back to School

School folders sit on the kitchen table; crisp new clothes are carefully laid out, and alarm clocks are set extra early. Hearts are racing with anticipation: tomorrow is the first day of school!

There are many things to do before school begins, including finishing up summer projects, planning the year's activities and vacations, and shopping.

Spending a day getting ready for the new year can be enjoyable, especially when you share it with your children. It's a time when everyone can discuss anxieties they may have, as well as anything else that needs to be discussed.

The recipes in this section were created to help make your new school year a good one. With so much going on, simplicity is the key.

Back-to-School Activities

1. Suggest that your children make lists to prepare for back-to-school shopping. One list may include school supplies; another may include clothes, shoes, undergarments, and coats.
2. Compare the lists and discuss whether buying new items is necessary. Have your children try on old clothes, and sort out clothes that can no longer be worn.
3. Help your children decide which items they need the most and want the most.
4. Take many breaks throughout your shopping day. You can use this time to discuss school and find out how your children feel about the new year.
5. Share meal preparation tasks, as this is a perfect way to spend time together and talk.

Things to Get Done

Back-to-School Menus

Hurry and Dress Breakfast

   Low-Fat Granola Cereal
* Frozen Fruit Compote
   Skim Milk

Best Buys Lunch

* LaVon's Cabbage Potato Soup
   Whole Wheat Dinner Rolls
* Vegetable Frittata with
   Low-Fat Creamy Celery Sauce
* Autumn Apple Bars
   Watermelon Wedges
   Skim Milk

Take-Your-Time Breakfast

* Crunchy French Toast
* Tropical Fruit Topping
   Skim Milk
   Coffee or Tea

(* recipe follows)

Hurry and Dress Breakfast Recipes

FROZEN FRUIT COMPOTE

1/2 cup sugar
1/3 cup orange juice
1/3 cup lemon juice concentrate
1/3 cup water
1/4 tsp. peppermint extract
8 cups assorted frozen fruit

Place fruit in a large shallow dish. Set aside. In a medium bowl, combine all ingredients except fruit; stir until sugar dissolves. Pour over fruit. Cover; chill 3 hours or overnight, stirring occasionally. Refrigerate leftovers. *Preparation time = 15 minutes. Refrigeration time = 3 hours.*

NUTRITION FACTS—Serving size = 1 cup • Servings = 8 • Calories = 116 • Total fat = <1 gm. • Cholesterol = 0 mg. • Sodium = 42 mg. • Total carbohydrate = 29 gm. • Dietary fiber = 0 gm. • Protein = 1 gm.

EXCHANGE VALUES—2 fruit

Best Buys Lunch Recipes

LAVON'S CABBAGE POTATO SOUP

3 cups cabbage, grated
2 cups potatoes, diced
1 med. onion, minced
2 cups water
1/2 tsp. salt
1/4 tsp. white pepper
1 1/2 cups skim milk
2 Tbsp. flour
2 Tbsp. low-fat tub margarine

Combine cabbage, potatoes, onion, water, salt, and pepper in saucepan. Cook for 15 minutes or until tender. Add 1 cup of milk, reserving 1/2 cup. Shake flour with remaining 1/2 cup milk in a toddy shaker. Add margarine to vegetable mixture, then slowly stir flour mixture into vegetables. Cook 3 to 5 minutes until desired consistency of soup is reached. Note: Any tight-lidded jar can function as an old-fashioned toddy shaker. *Preparation time = 30 minutes. Cooking time = 20 minutes.*

NUTRITION FACTS—Serving size = 1 cup • Servings = 6 • Calories = 138 • Total fat = 3 gm. • Cholesterol = 1 mg. • Sodium = 266 mg. • Total carbohydrate = 26 gm. • Dietary fiber = 4 gm. • Protein = 5 gm.

EXCHANGE VALUES—1 bread/starch, 2 vegetable

VEGETABLE FRITTATA WITH LOW-FAT CREAMY CELERY SAUCE

4 cups raw potato, chopped in blender
1 cup broccoli, chopped in blender
1 cup carrots, chopped in blender
1/2 cup onion, chopped in blender
2 tsp. garlic powder
1 tsp. savory
1 tsp. celery seed
1/2 tsp. white pepper
2 eggs (or 1/2 cup egg substitute) + 2 egg whites
2 Tbsp. flour
10 3/4 oz.-can low-fat cream of celery soup
1/4 cup skim milk
1 tsp. garlic powder
Nonstick cooking spray

Chop vegetables in blender; drain well. (You may want to press the water out of the vegetables, especially the potatoes.) Add garlic powder, savory, celery seed, and white pepper to the vegetables. Beat the eggs and egg whites. Fold into vegetable mixture. Stir flour into mixture. Spray a nonstick frying pan with nonstick cooking spray. To make individual frittatas, drop 1/2 cup of batter onto the hot pan and brown on both sides. While frittatas are frying, heat the cream of celery soup, skim milk, and garlic powder. Spoon over frittatas. *Preparation time = 30 minutes.*

NUTRITION FACTS—Serving size = 1 patty plus 2 Tbsp. of soup mixture • Servings = 8 • Calories = 227 • Total fat = 9 gm. • Cholesterol (with egg) = 55 mg. • Cholesterol (with egg substitute) = 1 mg. • Sodium = 177 mg. • Total carbohydrate= 33 gm. • Dietary fiber = 3 gm. • Protein = 5 gm.

EXCHANGE VALUES—1 medium-fat meat, 1 bread/starch, 3 vegetable

AUTUMN APPLE BARS

2/3 cup low-fat margarine
2 eggs (or 1/2 cup egg substitute)
1 cup brown sugar
1 tsp. vanilla
1 1/2 cups flour
1 tsp. baking soda
1/4 tsp. salt
1/2 cup walnuts
1 1/2 cups finely diced apples
Nonstick cooking spray

Preheat oven to 350°. Cream together margarine, eggs, brown sugar, and vanilla. Add dry ingredients, then fold in nuts and apples. Spray a 9" x 13" pan with nonstick cooking spray. Place mixture in pan and bake for 30 minutes. *Preparation time = 15 minutes. Baking time = 30 minutes.*

NUTRITION FACTS—Serving size = 1 bar • Servings = 18 • Calories = 158 • Total fat = 7 gm. • Cholesterol (with egg) = 24 mg. • Cholesterol (with egg substitute) = 0 mg. • Sodium = 98 mg. • Total carbohydrate = 23 gm. • Dietary fiber = <1 • Protein = 2 gm.

EXCHANGE VALUES—1 bread/starch, 1/2 fruit, 1 fat

Take-Your-Time Breakfast Recipes

CRUNCHY FRENCH TOAST

Arletta Giese of The Cunningham House in Platteville, Wisconsin, routinely serves this recipe. Dr. Cunningham was one of the first physicians in the Grant County area.

> 3 eggs (or 3/4 cup egg substitute)
> 1/2 cup skim milk
> 1/2 tsp. nutmeg
> 2 cups corn flakes
> 6 slices coarse white or wheat bread
> 1/4 cup low-fat margarine
> Waxed paper
> Nonstick cooking spray

Whisk eggs, milk, and nutmeg together until well blended. Pour into a soup bowl. Crush corn flakes and spread on a sheet of waxed paper. Dip both sides of bread into milk batter. Press both sides into corn flakes. Spray a nonstick skillet or griddle with nonstick cooking spray, and melt margarine as needed to grill bread on both sides until golden. (Hint: Keep warm by holding in a preheated oven at 200 to 225°.) *Preparation time = 15 minutes.*

NUTRITION FACTS—Serving size = 1 slice • Servings = 6 • Calories = 160 • Total fat = 6 gm. • Cholesterol (with egg) = 107 mg. • Cholesterol (with egg substitute) = <1 mg. • Sodium = 420 mg. • Total carbohydrate = 22 gm. • Dietary fiber = <1 gm. • Protein = 13 gm.

EXCHANGE VALUES—1 1/2 bread/starch, 1 fat

TROPICAL FRUIT TOPPING

3 Tbsp. lime juice
1/2 cup fresh pineapple chunks
1/2 cup papaya chunks
2 kiwifruit, peeled and chopped
1 Tbsp. honey
2 tsp. white wine vinegar

Combine all ingredients. Refrigerate 1 to 3 hours before serving. Serve with French toast. *Preparation time = 15 minutes. Refrigeration time = 1 hour.*

NUTRITION FACTS—Serving size = 1/4 cup • Servings = 4 • Calories = 63 • Total fat = <1 gm. • Cholesterol = 0 mg. • Sodium = 3 mg. • Total carbohydrate = 16 gm. • Dietary fiber = 2 gm. • Protein = <1 gm.

EXCHANGE VALUES—1 fruit

Back-To-School Shopping List

Take this book along to your supermarket or photocopy the list. Select the same number or size of items that you have in the past, based on the number of people for whom you are shopping. Review this list before you go to the store. Cross out items you have on hand, and write in your personal likes and needs.

Produce

Papaya
Watermelon
Apples
Limes
Pineapple
Kiwi
Cabbage
Potatoes
Onions
Broccoli
Carrots

Packaged

Low-fat granola cereal
Corn flakes
Walnuts
Coffee
Tea

Staples/Spices

Olive oil
Savory
Celery seed
Sugar
Brown sugar
Vanilla
Garlic powder
Nutmeg
Flour
Baking soda
Salt
White pepper
Peppermint extract

Bottled/Canned

Honey
White wine vinegar
Low-fat cream of celery soup
Lemon juice concentrate
Lime juice

Refrigerator Case

Skim milk
Eggs or egg substitute
Low-fat tub margarine
Orange juice

Bakery/Deli

Whole wheat dinner rolls
Course white or whole wheat
   bread

Frozen Case

Assorted frozen fruit

Other

Nonstick cooking spray
Waxed paper

County Fair

The smell of funnel cakes, cotton candy, and corn dogs; the roar of tractors; and the sound of three year olds "oohing" and "ahhing" at the 30-pound white bunny—the county fair is exciting for everyone!

The county fair, like the local farmers' market, brings together diverse individuals and cultures. Throughout history, the county fair has been the place for socializing, selling products, and exchanging innovative ideas.

Whether it's winning the prize teddy bear for your sweetheart, strolling hand-in-hand among the rides, or spotting that special person from the top of the Ferris wheel, this annual festival is always a hit!

County Fair Activities

1. Make plans early in the season to join a volleyball or softball team that will compete at the fair. This can be a fun and healthy activity for all family members.

2. As you travel to the fair, watch for roadside stands selling fresh produce. Compare the produce with exhibits at the fair.

3. Try to judge the weight of the animals on exhibit. Collect a small amount of money from each family member, then give the kitty to the family member who comes closest to guessing an animal's weight correctly.

County Fair Menus

Line Dancing BBQ

* Chutney-Style Pork Chops
* Pumpkin Bran Muffins
* Cindy and Patti's
  Green Bay Potatoes

Tossed Salad
Choice of Dressing
Skim Milk

Countryside Breakfast

Crusty Bagels
Nonfat Cream Cheese

Apple Juice
Coffee or Tea

Texas-Style Supper

* Cabbage and Raisin Stew
* Green Chilies Corn Bread
* Strawberry Pie

Skim Milk
Coffee or Tea

(* recipe follows)

Line Dancing BBQ Recipes

CHUTNEY-STYLE PORK CHOPS

4 pork chops
1/2 tsp. nutmeg
5-oz. container cranberry chutney
16-oz. can reduced-sugar sliced peaches
1 tsp. ginger
1 tsp. cinnamon

Preheat oven to 350°. Brown pork chops, seasoning them with nutmeg. Combine chutney, peaches, ginger, and cinnamon. Place browned pork chops in a casserole dish and pour chutney combination over them. Bake 30 minutes. *Preparation time = 15 minutes. Baking time = 30 minutes.*

NUTRITION FACTS—Serving size = 1 pork chop • Servings = 4 • Calories = 412 • Total fat = 9 gm. • Cholesterol = 91 mg. • Sodium = 100 mg. • Total carbohydrate = 29 gm. • Dietary fiber = 0 gm. • Protein = 26 gm.

EXCHANGE VALUES—4 lean meat, 1 bread/starch, 1 fruit, 1 fat

CINDY AND PATTI'S GREEN BAY POTATOES

2 lb. bag frozen Ore-Ida hashbrowns
16 oz. nonfat sour cream
10 3/4-oz. can Healthy Choice low-fat cream of mushroom soup
1/2 cup nonfat shredded cheddar cheese
Salt and pepper to taste
1/2 cup corn flakes, crushed
Nonstick cooking spray

Preheat oven to 350°. Combine the first five ingredients in a large bowl. Mix well. Bake in a baking dish sprayed with nonstick cooking spray for 30 minutes covered. Stir well. Top with corn flakes. Bake uncovered an additional 15 minutes. *Preparation time = 10 minutes. Baking time = 45 minutes.*

NUTRITION FACTS—Serving size = 1/2 cup • Servings = 6 • Calories = 135 • Total fat = 1 gm. • Cholesterol = 4 mg. • Sodium = 374 mg. • Total carbohydrate = 21 gm. • Dietary fiber = 2 gm. • Protein= 11 gm.

EXCHANGE VALUES—1 bread/starch, 1/2 skim milk

PUMPKIN BRAN MUFFINS

1 cup flour
1/4 cup bran buds
2 Tbsp. brown sugar
1 tsp. baking soda
1 tsp. cinnamon
1/2 tsp. salt
1/2 tsp. ginger
2 Tbsp. low-fat margarine
3/4 cup canned pumpkin
1 egg (or 1/4 cup egg substitute)
3/4 cup orange juice
1/3 cup walnuts, chopped
Nonstick cooking spray

Preheat oven to 350°. Combine first 7 ingredients and set aside. Mix margarine, pumpkin, egg, and orange juice together in medium-size bowl. Add dry ingredients, then fold in walnuts. Spray muffin tins with nonstick cooking spray. Bake 20 minutes. *Preparation time = 15 minutes. Baking time = 20 minutes.*

NUTRITION FACTS—Serving size = 1 muffin • Servings = 12 • Calories = 115 • Total fat = 6 gm. • Cholesterol (with egg) = 18 mg. • Cholesterol (with egg substitute) = 0 mg. • Sodium = 218 mg. • Total carbohydrate = 15 gm. • Dietary fiber = 3 gm. • Protein = 3 gm.

EXCHANGE VALUES—1 bread/starch, 1 fat

Texas-Style Supper Recipes

CABBAGE AND RAISIN STEW

7 cups chunked cabbage
2 1/2 cups sliced fresh mushrooms
1 cup chopped onions
1 cup red bell pepper, cut in julienne strips
2 cups water
1 cup raisins
2 tsp. chopped garlic
1 Tbsp. lemon juice
2 tsp. paprika
2 tsp. tarragon
1 Tbsp. low-fat margarine
1 Tbsp. flour
1/4 tsp. salt
1 cup skim milk

Cook cabbage, mushrooms, onions, bell peppers, water, raisins, garlic, lemon juice, paprika, and tarragon in a 2-quart saucepan on medium heat for 20 minutes. Simmer for an additional 20 minutes. Melt margarine in a small saucepan, then blend in flour and salt until smooth. Stir in cold milk gradually, and cook over direct heat, stirring constantly until flour mixture boils and becomes thick and smooth. Add this thin white sauce to stew mixture. Reheat, and serve. *Preparation time = 1 hour.*

NUTRITION FACTS—Serving size = 1 cup • Servings = 5 • Calories = 219 • Total fat = 3 gm. • Cholesterol = 0 mg. • Sodium = 198 mg. • Total carbohydrate = 48 gm. • Protein = 6 gm.

EXCHANGE VALUES—2 bread/starch, 2 vegetable

GREEN CHILIES CORN BREAD

1 cup yellow cornmeal
1 cup flour
1/4 cup sugar
2 1/2 tsp. baking powder
1/8 tsp. nutmeg
2 Tbsp. low-fat margarine
1 cup skim milk
2 egg whites
1 cup (4 oz.) nonfat cheddar cheese, shredded
2 Tbsp. canned diced green chilies, drained
Nonstick cooking spray

Preheat oven to 400°. Spray an 8" x 8" pan with nonstick cooking spray; set aside. In a large bowl, combine cornmeal, flour, sugar, baking powder, and nutmeg. In a medium bowl, mix together margarine, milk, and egg whites until smooth. Combine with cornmeal mixture until moist. Gently fold in cheese and chilies. Spoon into prepared pan. Bake for 20 to 25 minutes or until golden brown. Serve warm with honey. *Preparation time = 15 minutes. Baking time = 25 minutes.*

NUTRITION FACTS—Serving size = 1 piece • Servings = 12 • Calories = 158 • Total fat = 2 gm. • Cholesterol = <1 mg. • Sodium = 242 mg. • Total carbohydrate = 29 gm. • Dietary fiber = 1 gm. • Protein = 7 gm.

EXCHANGE VALUES—2 bread/starch

THINGS TO GET DONE

STRAWBERRY PIE

CRUST:

1/2 cup chopped pretzels
1/4 cup low-fat margarine
1/2 cup nonfat sour cream
3/4 cup flour

FILLING:

1 pkg. (3-oz.) sugar-free strawberry Jello
1 cup boiling water
2 cups sliced strawberries
1 small (8-oz.) container low-calorie whipped topping
Strawberry halves (for garnish)

Preheat oven to 350°. Chop pretzels in blender. Set aside. Cream margarine and sour cream, then add flour and chopped pretzels. Press into pie plate with fingers; flute edge. Bake 20 to 25 minutes.

Prepare Jello with 1 cup boiling water. When cool, add strawberries. When Jello starts to set, pour into cooled pie shell and frost with whipped topping. Garnish with strawberry halves. Note: Any fruit with corresponding flavor of Jello can be used. *Preparation time = 15 minutes. Baking time = 25 minutes.*

NUTRITION FACTS—Serving size = 1 piece • Servings = 6 • Calories = 162 • Total fat = 6 gm. • Cholesterol = 5 mg. • Sodium = 182 mg. • Total carbohydrate = 23 gm. • Dietary fiber = 2 gm. • Protein = 5 gm.

EXCHANGE VALUES—1 bread/starch, 1/2 fruit, 1 fat

County Fair Shopping List

Take this book along to your supermarket or photocopy the list. Select the same number or size of items that you have in the past, based on the number of people for whom you are shopping. Review this list before you go to the store. Cross out items you have on hand, and write in your personal likes and needs.

Produce

Red bell pepper
Lettuce
Strawberries
Cabbage
Mushrooms
Onions
Garlic

Packaged

Yellow cornmeal
Walnuts
Corn flakes
Sugar-free strawberry Jello
Coffee
Tea
Raisins

Staples/Spices

Tarragon
Flour
Brown sugar
Baking soda
Cinnamon
Salt
Baking powder
Ginger
Sugar
Nutmeg
Pepper
Paprika

Bottled/Canned

Reduced-sugar sliced peaches
Cranberry chutney
Healthy Choice low-fat cream of celery soup
Healthy Choice low-fat cream of mushroom soup
Honey
Lemon juice
Pumpkin
Apple juice
Salad dressing
Green chilies

Frozen Case

Orange juice
Low-calorie whipped topping
Frozen Ore-Ida hashbrowns

Refrigerator Case

Low-fat margarine
Eggs or egg substitute
Nonfat cream cheese
Skim milk
Nonfat shredded cheddar
   cheese
Nonfat sour cream

Meat Case

Pork chops

Bakery/Deli

Bagels

Snack Foods

Pretzels

Other

Nonfat cooking spray

Holiday Shopping

Colored lights decorate the tree; the sound of Nat King Cole's voice filters through your home, and thoughts of special gifts are on everyone's mind. It's time to give—and what better time to shop!

The holidays are a time to celebrate with family and friends, enjoy favorite foods, and take part in the joy of giving. This is an especially wonderful time for you and your loved ones to have fun together.

When it's time to go hunting for the perfect gift, it's nice to have delicious fare waiting for you when you return. The holiday recipes in this section have sold well in our family!

Holiday Shopping Activities

1. Ask everyone in your family to make a wish list—dreaming big is part of the fun. You may want to videotape this event to show relatives and to save for great memories.

2. Instead of writing out a shopping list of specific things each family member might want, write down a few of each person's interests, hobbies, or personal characteristics.

3. Try shopping at craft shows, antique malls, specialty boutiques, and off-the-beaten-path shops. Build a supply of mail-order catalogs to help you round out your shopping.

4. Use your creativity when wrapping presents. Sunday comics are a great way to wrap the gift for the comedian in your life, the Wall Street Journal works for the investment hobbyist, and sports magazine photos are just right for your sports enthusiast.

For the children on your list:

1. Let your children wrap gifts with paper from the ends of newspaper rolls, which is usually white or off white. They can use holiday stamps or they can draw and color holiday themes to decorate the packages. (Hint: The ends of newspaper rolls are found anywhere newspapers are printed.)
2. Consider lifetime gifts for children. Encourage them to begin a hobby or learn a new craft, and teach them what you know. Every Christmas, you can add to their special interest.

For children and adults:

1. Consider a personal gift by making coupons that the receiver can redeem later in the year. Some possibilities include a 15-minute back rub, cleaning a bedroom or the kitchen, breakfast in bed, or a specific number of wash loads.
2. Gifts of yourself work well for extended family and friends as well. For example, your children may enjoy a weekend at Uncle Dan's or an overnight with Aunt Ann.

Holiday Shopping Menus

Make a List Breakfast

* Apple Bran Oven Pancake
  Orange Juice
  Coffee or Tea

Talk Over the Great Bargains Lunch

* Low-Calorie Turkey-Spinach Lasagna
  Garlic Bread
  Fresh Pears
* Diane's Crazy Cake
* Danish Frosting
  Skim Milk

Holiday Wrapping Supper

* American Indian Stew
* Winter Rotini Salad
  Wax Beans
  Twelve Grain Bread

  Frozen Strawberry Yogurt
  Skim Milk
  Coffee or Tea

(* recipe follows)

Things to Get Done

Make a List Breakfast Recipes

APPLE BRAN OVEN PANCAKE

1/3 cup all-purpose flour
1/3 cup skim milk
2 eggs (or 1/2 cup liquid egg substitute)
2 tsp. sugar
1/8 tsp. salt
1/4 cup oat bran
1 tsp. low-fat margarine
1 medium apple, cored and thinly sliced
3 Tbsp. water
2 Tbsp. brown sugar
1/4 cup nonfat sour cream
1/2 tsp. cinnamon
1/2 tsp. vanilla
Apple slices (for garnish)

Preheat oven to 400°. In small mixer bowl, combine flour, milk, eggs, sugar, and salt; beat at medium speed until smooth (1 to 2 minutes). Stir in oat bran by hand. Set aside. Place margarine in a 9-inch glass pie pan and melt margarine in oven. Spread margarine evenly over bottom of pan. Pour oat bran mixture into prepared hot pan. Bake for 20 to 25 minutes or until pancake is puffed up and lightly browned. (Pancake will deflate when removed from oven.) Meanwhile, place apples and water in a 10-inch skillet. Cover; cook over medium heat until tender (3 to 4 minutes). Remove from heat; drain. Sprinkle with brown sugar. Cover, and let stand until sugar is melted. In a small bowl, stir together sour cream, cinnamon, and vanilla. Quickly spread the mixture in the center of the hot, baked pancake. Place apple slices on top in a circular pattern. To serve, cut into wedges. *Preparation time = 15 minutes. Baking time = 25 minutes.*

NUTRITION FACTS—Serving size = 1/6 of pancake • Servings = 6 • Calories = 132 • Total fat = 3 gm. • Cholesterol (with egg) = 71 mg. • Cholesterol (with egg substitute) = <1 mg. • Sodium = 88 mg. • Total carbohydrate = 21 gm. • Dietary fiber = <1 gm. • Protein = 6 gm.

EXCHANGE VALUES—1 bread/starch, 1 fruit

Talk Over the Great Bargains Lunch Recipes

LOW-CALORIE TURKEY-SPINACH LASAGNA

3 10-oz. boxes frozen chopped spinach
16 oz. low-fat ricotta cheese
2 cups cooked turkey, chopped
2 cups (or 1 15-oz.) jar spaghetti sauce
8 oz. low-fat mozzarella cheese, sliced
1/4 cup nonfat grated Parmesan cheese
Nonstick cooking spray

Preheat oven to 350°. Thaw spinach and squeeze out the liquid. Put about 1/3 of the spinach in the bottom of a casserole dish that has been sprayed lightly with nonstick cooking spray. Spread half of the ricotta over the spinach. Cover with half of the turkey. Spoon on half of the spaghetti sauce. Top with half of the mozzarella slices. Repeat the layering process using another third of the spinach; then the rest of the ricotta, turkey, spaghetti sauce, and mozzarella. Finish with the final third of spinach. Sprinkle on the Parmesan cheese. Bake for 45 to 50 minutes or until browned. *Preparation time = 30 minutes. Baking time = 50 minutes.*

NUTRITION FACTS—Serving size = 1/8 lasagna • Servings = 8 • Calories = 283 • Total fat = 10 gm. • Cholesterol = 85 mg. • Sodium = 450 mg. • Total carbohydrate = 13 gm. • Dietary fiber = <1 gm. • Protein = 36 gm. •

EXCHANGE VALUES—2 lean meat, 1 skim milk, 1/2 bread/starch, 1 fat

DIANE'S CRAZY CAKE

2 1/2 cups flour
1 1/2 cups sugar
1 tsp. salt
1 1/2 tsp. baking soda
1/4 cup unsweetened cocoa
1 tsp. vanilla
1 1/2 tsp. vinegar
1/2 cup canola oil
1 1/2 cup water

Preheat oven to 350°. Sift the first five ingredients into an ungreased 9" x 13" baking pan. Make 3 holes in the mixture. Put the vanilla in one hole, the vinegar in one hole, and the oil in the third hole. Pour 1 1/2 cups water over the top. Blend lightly with a fork. Do not beat. Bake 25 to 30 minutes until a toothpick comes out clean. Top with the Danish frosting on page 216. *Preparation time = 15 minutes. Baking time = 30 minutes.*

NUTRITION FACTS—Serving size = 1/12 of cake • Servings = 12 • Calories = 237 • Total fat = 5 gm. • Cholesterol = 0 mg. • Sodium = 336 mg. • Total carbohydrate = 46 gm. • Dietary fiber = <1 gm. • Protein = 3 gm. •

EXCHANGE VALUES—2 1/2 bread/starch, 1 fat

DANISH FROSTING

1/2 cup skim milk
3 tbsp. flour
1/2 cup low-fat margarine
1/2 cup sugar
1/4 tsp. salt
1 cup plus 2 Tbsp. powdered sugar
1 tsp. vanilla

Cook milk and flour together in a saucepan until thick. Place in refrigerator to cool. In a mixing bowl, beat margarine, sugar, and salt until fluffy. Add flour mixture and beat at high speed. Beat in sugar at high speed. Add vanilla. Frosts a 9" x 13" cake. *Preparation time = 10 minutes. Cooling time = 15 minutes. Cooking time = 10 minutes.*

NUTRITION FACTS—Serving size = 3 Tbsp. • Servings = 12 • Calories = 151 • Total fat = 4 gm. • Cholesterol = <1 mg. • Sodium = 157 mg. • Total carbohydrate = 30 gm. • Dietary fiber = <1 gm. • Protein = <1 gm.

EXCHANGE VALUES—1 1/2 bread/starch, 1/2 fat

NOTE: DIANE'S CRAZY CAKE AND DANISH FROSTING ARE NOT SUITABLE FOR MOST INDIVIDUALS FOLLOWING A DIET LOW IN SIMPLE SUGARS.

Holiday Wrapping Supper Recipes

AMERICAN INDIAN STEW

1/2 cup lentils, rinsed
1/2 cup navy beans, rinsed
2 cups chopped onion
2 cups chunked celery
5 carrots, scrubbed and chunked into 1-inch pieces
1/4 cup brown sugar
1 cup barley
1/2 tsp. thyme, chopped
1 tsp. chopped garlic
2 bay leaves
1 tsp. black pepper
1/2 cup red cooking wine
1 quart low-sodium V8 juice
2 cups water

Combine all ingredients in a Crockpot and cook for 8 to 10 hours on medium or low heat, or 4 to 5 hours on high heat. Remove bay leaves before serving. The flavor of this stew improves with time. For best results, prepare stew one to three days before serving. Keep refrigerated. Also, if more salt is desired, add salt at the end of cooking time. (Adding salt too soon can toughen the seed coats on the lentils.) *Preparation time = 15 minutes. Cooking time = 5 to 10 hours.*

NUTRITION FACTS—Serving size = 1 cup • Servings = 10 • Calories = 197 • Total fat = 1 gm. • Cholesterol = 0 mg. • Sodium = 99 mg. • Total carbohydrate = 41 gm. • Dietary fiber = 7 gm. • Protein = 4 gm.

EXCHANGE VALUES—2 bread/starch, 1 vegetable

THINGS TO GET DONE

WINTER ROTINI SALAD

3 cups rotini pasta
3 green onions, chopped
1 cup broccoli, chopped
10 ripe olives, sliced
1/2 cup cider vinegar
1/3 cup sugar
1/2 tsp. salt
1/4 tsp. white pepper
1 Tbsp. Mrs. Dash seasoning
2 medium tomatoes, peeled and chunked
2 Tbsp. fat-free Italian dressing
8 cherry tomatoes

Cook rotini in 4 cups of boiling water for 6 to 8 minutes. Drain and cool. Add onions, broccoli, and olives. Heat vinegar, sugar, salt, white pepper, and seasoning in a saucepan. Pour over vegetables. Stir in tomatoes and dressing. Refrigerate for one or more hours. Flavor improves if made the day before serving. Garnish with 8 cherry tomatoes. *Preparation time = 30 minutes. Refrigeration time = 1 hour.*

NUTRITION FACTS—Serving size = 1 cup • Servings = 8 • Calories = 141 • Total fat = 1 gm. • Cholesterol = 0 mg. • Sodium = 235 mg. • Total carbohydrate = 30 gm. • Dietary fiber = 3 gm. • Protein = 5 gm.

EXCHANGE VALUES—1 bread/starch, 2 vegetable

Holiday Shopping List

Take this book along to your supermarket or photocopy the list. Select the same number or size of items that you have in the past, based on the number of people for whom you are shopping. Review this list before you go to the store. Cross out items you have on hand, and write in your personal likes and needs.

Produce

Garlic
Broccoli
Onions
Green onions
Celery
Carrots
Tomatoes
Cherry tomatoes
Apples
Pears

Packaged

Barly
Oat bran
Lentils
Navy beans
Parmesan cheese, nonfat
Rotini
Coffee
Tea

Staples/Spices

White pepper
Black pepper
Salt
Mrs. Dash
Sugar
Powdered sugar
Brown sugar
Unsweetened cocoa
Thyme
Bay leaves
Baking soda
Vanilla
Cinnamon

Bottled/Canned

Wax beans
Ripe olives
Low-sodium V8 juice
Spaghetti sauce
Vinegar
Fat-free Italian dressing
Canola oil

Frozen Case

Chopped spinach
Orange juice
Frozen strawberry yogurt

Refrigerator Case

Low-fat ricotta cheese
Skim milk
Low-fat margarine
Eggs or egg substitute
Nonfat sour cream
Low-fat mozzarella cheese

Meat Case

Turkey

Bakery/Deli

Garlic bread
Twelve-grain bread

Other

Red cooking wine
Nonstick cooking spray

Healthy Choices

Home on the Range
•
Planning the Family Vacation
•
The Ecology Experience
•
White House Dining

HOME ON THE RANGE

The aroma of food on the grill pervades the warm air as children's faces radiate with excitement. Dinner is being prepared, and it won't be long before everyone can enjoy the flavors of the great outdoors!

Planning the first cookout usually begins with the first hint of spring. Whether you choose to have an outing in your backyard or in a nearby park, trying delicious grilled food while having fun with your family is a wonderful way to spend the day.

HOME ON THE RANGE ACTIVITIES

1. Make a date with your family, but be sure to schedule an alternate date in case of rain.

2. Buy a photo album or scrapbook. Take pictures of the first outing each year. You may want to have family members sign a page and encourage them to write down their feelings about the day. Include menus and recipes for next year's cookout.

3. Assign family members to make a list of equipment needed for the cookout. Make sure someone cleans the grill and washes picnic dishes that have been stored for several months.

4. Ask each family member to write down a favorite campfire story. Encourage family members to act out the story so other family members and friends can try to guess the story.

5. In case of rain, develop a menu of foods that can be eaten on a screened porch or in the house. Use a red-checkered tablecloth to make the meal seem like a picnic.

6. Use this time to talk about vacation plans for the summer. Draft a list with at least one suggestion from each person. Schedule tentative family meals or weekends to talk about any new vacation ideas.

Home on the Range Menus

Late Night Patio Party

   Deli Sub Sandwiches   Fresh Fruit
* Marie's Macaroni Salad   Skim Milk
* Dilly Green Beans   Coffee or Tea

Cookout Kickoff of the Season

   Grilled Chicken Breasts   Skim Milk
* Karen & Tony's All-   * Sharon's Patio Party
   Purpose BBQ Sauce   Vegetables
   Grilled Potatoes in Foil   Soft Drinks
   Grilled Texas Toast

Just Before Snipe Hunting

   Roasted Marshmallows
* Smores

(*recipe follows)

Healthy Choices

Late Night Patio Party Recipes

MARIE'S MACARONI SALAD

Marie Cull is my 88-year-old mother-in-law whom I love dearly. She still bakes bread twice a week. In fact, her grown children fight over the "inside" and "outside" rolls. She's one of the finest ladies I have had the privilege to get to know.

> *2 cups macaroni, cooked and drained on paper towel*
> *1/2 cup low-fat mayonnaise*
> *2 Tbsp. skim milk*
> *3/4 cup celery, chopped fine*
> *1/4 cup onion, chopped fine*
> *1/2 cup nonfat cheddar cheese, cubed*
> *1/4 tsp. salt*
> *1/4 tsp. pepper*

Combine all ingredients. Refrigerate 2 to 3 hours. Add more skim milk and low-fat mayonnaise if needed to make salad moist but not runny. *Preparation time = 15 minutes. Refrigeration time = 2 to 3 hours.*

NUTRITION FACTS—Serving size = 1/2 cup • Servings = 10 • Calories = 95 • Total fat = 1 gm. • Cholesterol = 2 mg. • Sodium = 192 mg. • Total carbohydrate = 16 gm. • Dietary fiber = 1 gm. • Protein = 6 gm.

EXCHANGE VALUES—1 bread/starch, 1 vegetable

DILLY GREEN BEANS

3 cups fresh green beans, cut French style and cooked
4-oz. can mushrooms, drained
1/2 cup sweet onion, sliced thin
1/2 tsp. dill weed
1 1/8 tsp. white pepper
1/2 cup cider vinegar
1/4 cup olive oil
1/4 cup sugar
1/2 cup sweet red pepper, chopped
1/4 tsp. salt

Combine the first five ingredients, and set aside. In a small saucepan, combine the vinegar, olive oil, sugar, red pepper, and salt. Boil for 2 minutes. When cool, pour over vegetables and refrigerate for 6 or more hours. *Preparation time = 15 minutes. Refrigeration time = 6 hours.*

NUTRITION FACTS—Serving size = 1/2 cup • Servings = 8 • Calories = 46 • Total fat = <1 gm. • Cholesterol = 0 mg. • Sodium = 74 mg. • Total carbohydrate = 11 gm. • Dietary fiber = <1 gm. • Protein = 1 gm.

EXCHANGE VALUES—2 vegetable

Cookout Kickoff of the Season Recipes

KAREN AND TONY'S ALL-PURPOSE BBQ SAUCE

Karen and Tony are two of my oldest and dearest friends.

> 1 Tbsp. canola oil
> 1 clove garlic, minced very fine
> 1/2 cup catsup
> 1/3 cup chili sauce
> 2 Tbsp. brown sugar
> 1 tsp. lemon juice
> 2 Tbsp. onion flakes
> 1 Tbsp. Worcestershire sauce
> 1 Tbsp. prepared mustard
> Crushed black pepper or cayenne to taste

Combine all ingredients and bring to a boil. Simmer for 10 to 15 minutes until flavors have melded (or, as Tony says, "Nurse it along and don't leave your post"). This is an adequate amount of sauce for about 4 pounds of ribs or 12 chicken breasts. Note: If you need to watch your salt intake because of high blood pressure, go very easy on this sauce. Use just enough to get the barbecue flavor. *Preparation time = 30 minutes.*

NUTRITION FACTS—Serving size = 2 Tbsp. • Servings = 24 • Calories = 21 • Total fat = <1 gm. • Cholesterol = 0 mg. • Sodium = 112 mg. • Total carbohydrate = 4 gm. • Dietary fiber = <1 gm. • Protein = <1 gm.

EXCHANGE VALUES—1/2 bread/starch

SHARON'S PATIO PARTY VEGETABLES

My friend Sharon entertains with her red dishes and many candles. This vegetable dish is a favorite at her dinner parties.

2 10-oz. bags of frozen broccoli cuts
2 cups frozen small, whole onions
  (or 3 medium onions, quartered)
1/2 cup low-fat margarine
2 Tbsp. flour
1/4 tsp. salt
Dash of pepper
1 cup skim milk
1/4 cup nonfat cream cheese
1/2 cup nonfat sharp cheddar cheese, shredded
1 cup soft bread crumbs
Nonstick cooking spray

Preheat oven to 350°. Cook broccoli as directed on package. Drain. Cook onions in boiling water until tender. Drain. In a saucepan, melt half of the margarine. Blend in flour, salt, and pepper. Add milk. Cook, stirring constantly until thickened and bubbly. Reduce heat; blend in cream cheese until smooth. Spray a 1 1/2 quart casserole dish with nonstick cooking spray. Layer vegetables in dish. Pour sauce mixture over, and mix lightly. Top with cheese. Melt the remaining margarine and toss with bread crumbs. Sprinkle on top of casserole. Bake for 40 to 45 minutes. *Preparation time = 15 minutes. Baking time = 45 minutes.*

NUTRITION FACTS—Serving size = 3/4 cup • Servings = 8 • Calories = 188 • Total fat = 7 gm. • Cholesterol = 2 mg. • Sodium = 405 mg. • Total carbohydrate = 25 gm. • Dietary fiber = 1 gm. • Protein = 9 gm.

EXCHANGE VALUES—1 bread/starch, 2 vegetable, 1 fat

Just Before Snipe Hunting Recipe

SMORES

> 2 chocolate bars, cut in half
> 4 marshmallows
> 8 graham cracker halves

Toast marshmellows. Place half of a chocolate bar and one toasted marshmallow between two graham cracker halves. Press together firmly. Use long handled tongs to hold over the campfire. Enjoy!

NUTRITION FACTS—Serving size = 1 sandwich • Servings = 4 • Calories = 212 • Total fat = 8 gm. • Cholesterol = 0 mg. • Sodium = 108 mg. • Total carbohydrate = 32 gm. • Dietary fiber = 0 gm. • Protein = 3 gm.

EXCHANGE VALUES—2 bread/starch, 1 1/2 fat

NOTE: THIS RECIPE MAY NOT BE SUITABLE FOR INDIVIDUALS FOLLOWING A DIET LOW IN SIMPLE SUGARS.

Home on the Range Shopping List

Take this book along to your supermarket or photocopy the list. Select the same number or size of items that you have in the past, based on the number of people for whom you are shopping. Review this list before you go to the store. Cross out items you have on hand, and write in your personal likes and needs.

Produce

Fruit
Celery
Onions
Sweet onion
Potatoes
Green beans
Red pepper
Garlic

Packaged

Marshmallows
Graham crackers
Macaroni
Coffee
Tea

Staples/Spices

Onion flakes
Salt
Sugar
Black pepper
White pepper

Flour
Olive oil
Canola oil
Dill weed
Brown sugar
Cayenne pepper
Worcestershire sauce

Bottled/Canned

Prepared mustard
Low-fat mayonnaise
Catsup
Mushrooms
Lemon juice
Cider vinegar
Chili sauce

Frozen Case

Frozen small whole onions

Refrigerator Case

Skim milk
Nonfat sharp cheddar cheese
Low-fat margarine
Nonfat cream cheese

Meat Case

Chicken breasts

Bakery/Deli

Texas toast
Sub sandwiches
Bread (for soft bread crumbs)

Snack Foods

Chocolate bars

Other

Soft drinks
Nonstick cooking spray
Aluminum foil

Planning the Family Vacation

The beach is heavenly in the moonlight; the amusement park takes our breath away; the mountains are pristine and so green; the museums are extraordinary. If only we could decide on our vacation destination for the year!

Choosing the family vacation spot isn't always easy, especially when there are so many wonderful places to go in the world. But when you do decide (probably after some compromising), it will go smoothly if you start planning right away!

In this section are ways to help you and your family plan your vacation. While you're planning, there are some great recipes you can enjoy together, too.

Planning the Family Vacation Activities

1. Ideas to help you plan ahead:

    - Pack appropriate clothes for the place you're visiting.

    - Make reservations well in advance. Get confirmation numbers for hotels/motels/bed and breakfasts. Make sure that a late check-in will be okay.

    - If you travel by car, schedule time for frequent stops.

2. Gift wrap travel games for the children so they can have little surprises along the way. Car bingo, activity books, mini writing boards, magnetic travel games, and journals are all possibilities. These packages could also be used to reward children for their good behavior, such as helping out with travel chores. (Hint: Reward often, especially with young children.) And don't for-

get to pack a young child's favorite toy and favorite blanket or a pillow.

3. Play travel games! Find roadside signs that have words that begin with each successive letter of the alphabet; the person who completes the alphabet first wins. If you're traveling cross-country, find license plates for as many of the 50 states as you can; the person who finds the most in the allotted time wins!

4. Make lists that organize every detail of your trip. This can take the pressure off and help avoid last minute frustrations.

Plan the Family Vacation Menus

Across the World Supper

* Italian Pork Chops	Multi-Grain Biscuits
* Squash Mountains	Soft-Serve Yogurt
Cherry Tomatoes	Low-Fat Chocolate Milk

Lunch Around the Globe

* Virginia's Broccoli and Rice	Red Delicious Apples
Yellow Wax Beans	Skim Milk
French Bread	

Travel the USA Breakfast

Microwave Waffles

Fruit Spread

Freshly Squeezed Orange Juice

(* recipe follows)

Across the World Recipes

ITALIAN PORK CHOPS

2 lb. lean pork, cut into julienne strips
1 Tbsp. olive oil
3/4 tsp. nutmeg
1 yellow pepper, cut into julienne strips
1 medium onion, thinly sliced
10 3/4-oz. can low-sodium chicken broth
2 cups Healthy Choice Italian-style vegetable pasta sauce
2 medium zucchini, sliced thin
3/4 cup uncooked converted rice
1/2 tsp. white pepper
1/2 tsp. marjoram
1 tsp. garlic powder
1 Tbsp. low-sodium soy sauce
1 Tbsp. brown sugar
Nonstick cooking spray

Preheat oven to 350°. Brown pork strips in olive oil and nutmeg in nonstick frying pan. Remove browned pork from frying pan and set aside. Sauté pepper and onion for about 5 minutes. Stir in chicken broth, pasta sauce, rice, remaining spices, and brown sugar. Heat thoroughly. Spray a casserole dish with nonstick cooking spray. Layer pork strips in casserole dish, then place zucchini slices on top, and pour pasta mixture over the top. Bake for 45 minutes. Sprinkle with soy sauce just before serving. *Preparation time = 20 minutes. Baking time = 45 minutes.*

NUTRITION FACTS—Serving size = 1 pork chop • Servings = 8 • Calories = 227 • Total fat = 16 gm. • Cholesterol = 54 mg. • Sodium = 266 mg. • Total carbohydrate = 6 gm. • Dietary fiber = <1 gm. • Protein = 13 gm.

EXCHANGE VALUES—2 medium fat meat, 1 vegetable, 1 fat

SQUASH MOUNTAINS

Butternut squash
4 Tbsp. flour
1 tsp. garlic powder
1/2 tsp. onion powder
1 Tbsp. olive oil
1/2 tsp. white pepper
1/2 cup skim milk
2 tsp. dill weed

Cut 6 half-slices from the solid end of butternut squash; remove rind. Dredge pieces of "squash meat" in mixture of flour, garlic powder, and onion powder. Using a nonstick skillet, brown squash in olive oil, adding white pepper after both sides are browned. Remove from skillet and cut into chunks. Set aside. In skillet, combine remaining flour mixture with skim milk. Return squash to skillet and pour flour mixture over squash. Heat until slightly thickened. Sprinkle with dill weed just before serving. *Preparation time = 30 minutes.*

NUTRITION FACTS—Serving size = 1/2 cup • Servings = 6 • Calories = 90 • Total fat = 3 gm. • Cholesterol = <1 mg. • Sodium = 15 mg. • Total carbohydrate = 16 gm. • Dietary fiber = <1 gm. • Protein = 2 gm.

EXCHANGE VALUES—1 bread/starch

Lunch Around the Globe Recipes

VIRGINIA'S BROCCOLI AND RICE CASSEROLE

2 ribs celery, chunked
3/4 cup chopped onion
1/4 cup low-fat margarine
16-oz. frozen broccoli cuts
10 3/4-oz. can low-fat cream of mushroom soup
10 3/4-oz. can low-fat cream of chicken soup
4-oz. can sliced water chestnuts
1/2 tsp. white pepper
1 cup nonfat shredded cheddar cheese
Nonstick cooking spray

Preheat oven to 350°. Spray casserole dish with nonstick cooking spray. Sauté celery and onion in margarine in nonstick skillet. Combine remaining ingredients in a bowl, reserving 1/2 cup cheese. Add sautéed mixture and stir. Place mixture in dish. Sprinkle remaining 1/2 cup cheese on top. Bake for 40 to 45 minutes. *Preparation time = 15 minutes. Baking time = 45 minutes.*

NUTRITION FACTS—Serving size = 1 cup • Servings = 8 • Calories = 123 • Total fat = 5 gm. • Cholesterol = 6 mg. • Sodium = 475 mg. • Total carbohydrate = 13 gm. • Dietary fiber = 3 gm. • Protein = 8 gm.

EXCHANGE VALUES—1 bread/starch, 1 fat

Family Vacation Shopping List

Take this book along to your supermarket or photocopy the list. Select the same number or size of items that you have in the past, based on the number of people for whom you are shopping. Review this list before you go to the store. Cross out items you have on hand, and write in your personal likes and needs.

Produce

Cherry tomatoes
Oranges
Celery
Onions
Butternut squash
Yellow pepper
Red delicious apples
Zucchini

Packaged

Macaroni
Converted rice

Staples/Spices

Dill weed
Black pepper
White pepper
Olive oil
Flour
Garlic powder
Onion powder
Nutmeg
Marjoram
Brown sugar
Low-sodium soy sauce

Bottled/Canned

Low-sodium chicken broth
Low-fat cream of mushroom soup
Low-fat cream of chicken soup
Yellow wax beans
Water chestnuts
Healthy Choice Italian-style pasta sauce
Fruit spread

Frozen Case

Broccoli
Microwave waffles

Refrigerator Case

Low-fat margarine
Nonfat grated cheddar cheese
Skim milk
Low-fat chocolate milk

Meat Case

Lean pork

Bakery/Deli

Multi-grain biscuits
French bread

Other

Soft-serve yogurt
Nonstick cooking spray

The Ecology Experience

As we walk through the sharp grass, the trees seem to be saying something to us. The mountains and streams radiate with a natural energy. Everything is so alive in nature!

When the weather is warm, it's fun to take an evening walk or a late-afternoon picnic in the park to enjoy the beauty outside. Children especially like to discover nature; every tree, flower, and animal is unique.

If you're picnicking, take a couple of our recipes along with a fresh herb or vegetable from your own garden. It's easy to thrive in this environment!

The Ecology Experience Activities

1. Plant an edible herb or flower garden. Herbs flourish in traditional gardens as well as apartment patio planters or clay pots indoors.
2. List recipes your family would like to try. Make a second list of the spices, herbs, flowers, and vegetables that you can plant to use in these recipes.
3. Smell and taste small samples of the spices and herbs from a local health store co-op.
4. Sketch an herb garden you would like to plant. If you are interested, include herbs unfamiliar to you.
5. Plant and water your garden; watch it grow.
6. Pick herbs or flowers to use in the recipes you have chosen.

Herbs to Learn About

1. LAVENDER—Lilac-colored flowers; makes aromatic sachets when dried.
2. DILL—Used in pickling and flavoring fish, potatoes, and other vegetables, and in many vegetable dips.
3. SAGE—Blue flowers with broad leaves. Used to season poultry stuffing, meats, and sausages.
4. PARSLEY—An herb used to garnish and add flavor to soups and other dishes; contains some beta-carotene, so it's good for you besides tasting good.
5. LAVENDER VERA—A garden favorite with an attractive gray-green foliage.
6. SWEET WOODRUFF—A plant with small star-shaped blossoms. Can be used in teas, and is an excellent ground cover.
7. THYME—Excellent for flavoring lamb and other meats. Adds excitement to many vegetable dishes.
8. CUMIN—Seeds are often used in flavoring curries.
9. CILANTRO—A very common seasoning in many cuisines, especially Tex-Mex; similar to parsley.
10. OREGANO—Has thick green leaves and lavender-pink flowers; used in Italian dishes.
11. MINT—Oil is used to flavor peppermint candies and tea.
12. SORREL—Used to add flavor to salads and soups.
13. CHIVES—An onion-flavored herb for flavoring and garnishing soups, potatoes, and salads.
14. BASIL—Has tender, sweet leaves; a fragrant friend of the tomato.
15. BORAGE—This blue-flowered herb has a cucumber flavor.
16. CHAMOMILE—Has strong-scented foliage; flowers are used in teas, some of which are considered medicinal.

17. ROSEMARY—A sub-shrub with pale blue flowers. Used in salads and for seasoning pork and lamb.
18. NASTURTIUM—Has jewel-like blossoms held well above the deep green leaves. Edible flowers may be used in salads.
19. FENNEL—Grows four feet tall. Leaves are used in fish sauces and for garnishing.
20. LEMON MINT (OR MONARDA CITRIODORA)—Has lemon-scented leaves and flowers that attract bees. The oil was used by North American natives as a medicine for wounds.

THE ECOLOGY EXPERIENCE MENUS

BIRDER'S BREAKFAST

* Low Cholesterol Popovers   Apple Juice
* Raspberry Jello Loaf   Skim Milk

"CELEBRATE YOUR HABITAT" PICNIC IN THE PARK

* Kohlrabi Casserole   Rome Apples
* Nasturtium Salad   Skim Milk
  Whole Grain Bread   Coffee or Tea

SUPPER BY THE RIVER

* John and Sally's Wild Rice   * Strawberry Tofu
  Stuffed Peppers   Smoothies
* Granny's Mud Pie   Skim Milk
  Garlic Bread Sticks

(* recipe follows)

Birder's Breakfast Recipes

POPOVERS

1/2 cup whole wheat flour
1/2 cup unbleached white flour
1/4 tsp. salt
1 cup skim milk
1 egg (or 1/4 cup liquid egg substitute)
1 egg white
Nonstick cooking spray

Preheat oven to 425°. Spray muffin or popover tins with nonstick cooking spray and preheat. Combine all the ingredients in a bowl. Beat with a rotary beater or wire whisk just until smooth. Pour the batter into the heated muffin tins. Bake for 35 to 45 minutes or until brown. *Preparation time = 10 minutes. Baking time = 45 minutes.*

NUTRITION FACTS—Serving size = 1 popover • Servings = 9 • Calories = 68 • Total fat = 1 gm. • Cholesterol = 32 mg. • Sodium = 82 mg. • Total carbohydrate = 11 gm. • Dietary fiber = 0 gm. • Protein = 3 gm.

EXCHANGE VALUES—1 bread/starch

RASPBERRY JELLO LOAF

1/2 cup water
15 1/4-oz. can crushed pineapple
 (drain and save 1/2 cup juice)
3-oz. package sugar-free raspberry gelatin
1 cup red raspberries
1 cup low-fat whipped topping
Nonstick cooking spray
6 red raspberries (for garnish)

Heat water and pineapple juice until boiling. Add gelatin and stir until dissolved (about 2 minutes). Pour 3/4 cup gelatin mixture into a loaf pan that has been sprayed with nonstick cooking spray. Refrigerate for 30 minutes or until gelatin starts to set. Meanwhile, combine rest of gelatin mixture with pineapple, raspberries, and whipped topping. Pour into loaf pan. Refrigerate. When loaf has started to mold, add rest of gelatin mixture. Refrigerate for several hours. Unmold and garnish with whipped topping and raspberries. *Preparation time = 45 minutes. Refrigeration time = 1 hour.*

NUTRITION FACTS—Serving size = 1/2 cup • Servings = 6 • Calories = 89 • Total fat = 2 gm. • Cholesterol = 5 mg. • Sodium = 14 mg. • Total carbohydrate = 17 gm. • Dietary fiber = 0 gm. • Protein 2 gm.

EXCHANGE VALUES—1 1/2 fruit

"Celebrate Your Habitat" Picnic in the Park Recipes

KOHLRABI CASSEROLE

2-3 medium kohlrabi, peeled and cubed (2 1/2 cups)
1 medium carrot, sliced
3 oz. Canadian bacon
1 tsp. Dijon mustard
2 tsp. crushed garlic
2 tsp. thyme
Unsalted croutons, to taste

FOR MOCK CREAM SOUP:
2 cups nonfat dry milk
3/4 cup cornstarch
2 tsp. Mrs. Dash seasoning
Nonstick cooking spray

Preheat oven to 350°. To prepare the mock cream soup, mix dry milk, cornstarch, and Mrs. Dash thoroughly, and store in a covered container until ready to use. To prepare casserole, place kohlrabi and carrot in a microwaveable container with 3 cups water; cover and microwave on high power for 10 minutes. Drain juice and save. Cut Canadian bacon into 1 1/2-inch strips. Combine 2/3 cup of prepared mock cream soup with 2 1/3 cups of juice drained from vegetables. Cook in saucepan until thickened; add kohlrabi, carrot, bacon, mustard, garlic, and thyme. Spray a 5 1/2" x 8 1/2" casserole dish with nonstick cooking spray. Place mixture in dish and sprinkle with croutons. Bake for an hour. Turn off oven but keep dish in oven for 10 more minutes to allow ingredients to settle before serving. *Preparation time – 20 minutes. Baking time – 1 hour and 10 minutes.*

NUTRITION FACTS—Serving size = 1/2 cup • Servings = 6 • Calories = 88 • Total fat = 2 gm. • Cholesterol = 9 mg. • Sodium = 306 mg. • Total carbohydrate = 13 gm. • Dietary fiber = 2 gm. • Protein = 7 gm.

EXCHANGE VALUES—1 bread/starch

NASTURTIUM SALAD

My sister, Carol, is the "Martha Stewart" of my family. She designed the flower and herb gardens at the Parson's Inn. Her Christmas presents are elegantly wrapped. This is her recipe.

> 1 bunch arugula greens
> 1 small red onion, sliced and divided into rings
> 10 button mushrooms, sliced
> 1 medium tomato, cut into wedges
> 12 nasturtium blossoms
> 1 Tbsp. Dijon mustard
> 1/4 tsp. salt
> 1/4 tsp. coarse pepper
> 3 Tbsp. white wine vinegar
> 2 Tbsp. olive oil

Wash and dry arugula greens. Tear by hand and place in salad bowl. Add onions, mushrooms, and tomato. Toss briefly. Divide into individual salad bowls. Add nasturtium blossoms to salads, using them as garnish. Refrigerate until time to serve. For dressing, whisk together mustard, salt, pepper, and white wine vinegar. Slowly add oil and whisk until combined. Pour into a cruet, and serve with salad. *Preparation time = 10 minutes.*

NUTRITION FACTS—Serving size = 1 cup • Servings = 6 • Calories = 60 • Total fat = 5 gm. • Cholesterol = 0 mg. • Sodium = 136 mg. • Total carbohydrate = 4 gm. • Dietary fiber = <1 gm. • Protein = 1 gm.

EXCHANGE VALUES—1 vegetable, 1 fat

STRAWBERRY TOFU SMOOTHIES

1/2 cup unsweetened pineapple juice
2 cups fresh or frozen strawberries
   (if fresh, save 4 with stems for garnish)
6 ice cubes
2 kiwifruit, peeled and sliced (save 4 slices
   for garnish)
1 package tofu, drained (1 cup)

Combine all ingredients in a blender and puree until smooth. Pour into champagne or other stemmed glasses. Serve garnished with a kiwi slice and a strawberry. *Preparation time = 15 minutes.*

NUTRITION FACTS—Serving size = 1 cup • Servings = 4 • Calories = 157 • Total fat = 3 gm. • Cholesterol = 0 mg. • Sodium = 13 mg. • Total carbohydrate = 18 gm. • Dietary fiber = 5 gm. • Protein = 11 gm.

EXCHANGE VALUES—1/2 bread, 1 lean meat, 1 fruit

Supper by the River Recipes

JOHN AND SALLY'S WILD RICE STUFFED PEPPERS

It would be difficult to say whose peppers are best. Sally would probably say John learned to make them from her!

4 large green peppers
1/2 lb. 93% fat-free ground beef
1 cup chopped onion
2 cups tomato sauce
1 tsp. Worcestershire sauce
2 cloves garlic, minced
1/2 tsp. salt
1/2 tsp. pepper
1 cup long-grain wild rice

Preheat oven to 350°. Cut the tops off of the peppers; remove seeds and membranes. Wash in cold water. Brown ground beef. Drain. Add remaining ingredients. Stuff peppers lightly with mixture. Stand peppers upright in baking dish. Add 1/4 inch of water to bottom of dish. Bake covered 1 1/2 to 2 hours. *Preparation time = 20 minutes. Baking time = 2 hours.*

NUTRITION FACTS—Serving size = 1 pepper • Servings = 4 • Calories = 358 • Total fat = 10 gm. • Cholesterol = 56 mg. • Sodium = 355 mg. • Total carbohydrate = 46 gm. • Dietary fiber = 4 gm. • Protein = 23 gm.

EXCHANGE VALUES—2 medium fat meat, 2 bread/starch, 1 fat

GRANNY'S MUD PIE

Try serving this dessert in clay flower pots complete with gummy worms and artificial flowers. Clay pots can be used as table favors for each guest.

> 1 1/2 cups crushed Snackwell low-fat chocolate cookies (18 cookies)
> 2 Tbsp. liquid egg substitute
> 5 cups low-fat frozen chocolate yogurt
> 1 cup low-fat whipped topping
> Nonstick cooking spray
> Aluminum foil (if serving in clay pots)

Preheat oven to 375°. Spray a 9-inch round pie pan with nonstick cooking spray. Set aside. Mix 1 cup of crushed cookies with egg substitute until thoroughly moistened. Press the mixture into the bottom of the pie pan. Bake for 15 minutes. Let cool. Fill the pie shell with chocolate yogurt. Spread whipped topping on yogurt. Sprinkle remaining cookie crumbs on top of pie. Freeze for at least 3 hours before serving. Hint: If serving mud pie in clay pots, scrub pots, spray with nonstick cooking spray, and line bottom of pots with aluminum foil. *Preparation and baking time = 30 minutes. Freezing time = 3 hours.*

NUTRITION FACTS—Serving size = 1/10th of pie • Servings = 10 • Calories = 134 • Total fat = 6 gm. • Cholesterol = 3 mg. • Sodium = 222 mg. • Total carbohydrate = 19 gm. • Dietary fiber = <1 gm. • Protein = 1 gm.

EXCHANGE VALUES—1 bread/starch, 1 fat

Ecology Experience Shopping List

Take this book along to your supermarket or photocopy the list. Select the same number or size of items that you have in the past, based on the number of people for whom you are shopping. Review this list before you go to the store. Cross out items you have on hand, and write in your personal likes and needs.

Produce

Red raspberries
Arugula greens
Onions
Red onions
Kohlrabi
Carrots
Garlic
Mushrooms
Tomato
Strawberries
Kiwi
Green peppers
Nasturtium blossoms
Rome apples

Packaged

Snackwell low-fat chocolate
    cookies
Unsalted croutons
Nonfat dry milk
Sugar-free
    raspberry gelatin
Long-grain wild rice

Coffee
Tea

Staples/Spices

Mrs. Dash seasoning
Olive oil
Black pepper
Coarse pepper
Flour
Whole wheat flour
Salt
Thyme
Cornstarch
Cloves

Bottled/Canned

Crushed pineapple
Pineapple juice, unsweetened
Apple juice
White wine vinegar
Dijon mustard
Tomato sauce
Worcestershire sauce

Frozen Case

Low-fat frozen chocolate
  yogurt
Low-fat whipped topping

Refrigerator Case

Low-fat margarine
Eggs of egg substitute
Skim milk
Tofu

Meat Case

Canadian bacon
93% fat-free ground beef

Bakery/Deli

Whole grain bread
Garlic bread sticks

Other

Nonstick cooking spray

WHITE HOUSE DINING

Dinner is served! Just as it was in the late 18th century, this nine-course meal looks and smells like heaven—so elegant, so splendid. What a wonderful evening of dinner, candlelight, and conversation.

Families and lifestyles have changed since then (as well as the number of dinner courses), but there's always time for a special dinner the entire family can enjoy together.

As a fun way to promote conversation, we choose two or three topics to talk about during dinner. It can be a current issue or a family topic, or anything for that matter—just so it's interesting and enjoyable to discuss.

Whatever conversation you choose to indulge in, the recipes in this section will be a perfect complement!

WHITE HOUSE DINING ACTIVITIES

1. Choose favorite topics to begin family conversation at your semiformal dinner. You can choose almost any topic, as long as all family members are comfortable and interested in it. You may want to take this opportunity to discuss current events from a variety of family perspectives.

2. Assign one family member to be the server. He or she will present the foods that will be passed around the table or dished out in the kitchen.

3. Choose a centerpiece that will not block table talk. Any arrangement should be six inches or shorter. A bouquet of flowers that blend in with your color scheme is a great idea. For alternate centerpieces, consider small mementos from a trip, favorite framed pictures, or a bowl of fresh fruit.

4. Look at the information on page 254 to learn how to set a formal table. If someone in the family is a pro at table setting, it would be ideal to have that person teach other family members.

5. Borrow or buy a guidebook to Washington, D.C., and look for pictures or diagrams of the rooms in the White House. Imagine your family eating together in the formal dining room.

6. You may want to take some photos as keepsakes for you and your guests.

White House Dining Menus

Semi-Formal State Dinner

* Sesame-Soy Cod
* Twice-Baked Potatoes
* Cherry-Coke Salad
   Asti Spumanti
   Non-Alcoholic Champagne

   Crusty Warm Dinner Rolls
* Flaming Bananas Foster
   Skim Milk
   Coffee or Tea

Oval Office Breakfast

* Presidential Flannel Cakes
   Warm Maple Syrup
   Skim Milk

   Orange Juice
   Coffee or Tea

Cream Tea With the First Lady

* Oatmeal Raisin Scones
* Carrot Sandwiches
* Mamie Eisenhower Fudge
* Frannie's Maids of Honor
   Low-Fat Whipped Topping

   Raspberry Fruit Spread
   Sugar Cubes
   Cream or Cream Substitute
   Lemon Slices
   Apricot Herbal Tea

(* recipe follows)

Healthy Choices

SETTING YOUR WHITE HOUSE TABLE

Formal table setting has some basic guidelines. Ask the children to set the table, using these rules.

1. Line up all handles of silverware and the edge of the plate an inch from the table edge.

2. Place knife and spoon to the right of the plate. The knife is closest to the plate with the knife blade facing the plate. The spoon is placed to the right of the knife.

3. Place the fork or forks to the left of the plate. If your meal has two or more courses, you will place the fork that you use first to the outside.

4. Napkins may be placed at the left of the fork. They should not be under the fork. The diner should be able to place the napkin in his or her lap before picking up the fork. The open corner of the napkin should be closest to the fork. When the diner picks up the napkin by that corner, the napkin should neatly fall open.

5. The beverage glass is placed at the point of the knife and several inches back. If wine is served, these glasses are placed in the order of use, beginning at the point of the knife.

6. If desired, you can place a butter plate at the point of the fork, and several inches from the fork.

7. If you serve dessert, you will want to clear the dinner plate and replace it with the dessert plate. If you have a silverware crunch, just rewash the salad fork and serve the clean fork with dessert.

8. If coffee or tea is served, the cup and saucer can be placed to the right of the knife. You will need to provide a clean spoon for guests who use cream or sugar.

Cream Tea Etiquette

Cream tea is served at 4 in the afternoon. High tea traditionally was served later, at 6 or 7 p.m. The name high tea originally was used because the tea drinkers sat on high stools.

Certain rules of etiquette apply at a formal cream tea.

- Tea is not served like coffee. The person hosting the tea is seated at a table with the tea service placed in front of him or her.
- The tea service consists of a gleaming silver tray that is not covered by a cloth. On the tray is a teapot, a pitcher of cream, cubes of sugar in a bowl, a cake knife, sugar tongs, and thin slices of lemon on a plate.
- If there is space, the teacups and a stack of saucers, with a folded napkin between each saucer, are placed on the tray. A pot of boiling water should be available for those who wish to dilute the tea to make it weaker. Some guests would appreciate a decaffeinated tea, as well.
- Each guest moves through the tea line and is served a cup of tea.
- Refills are available when desired.
- Guests are offered a selection of dainty sandwiches, scones, crumpets, cookies, cakes, and fruits. Whipped cream, clotted cream, butter, jams, and jellies are available as spreads and toppings. To improve the nutritional value of "cream" tea, serve 2 percent milk instead of cream, fruit spreads instead of jellies and jams, and low-fat margarine instead of butter.

How to Brew Perfect Tea

- Allow water to boil 3 to 5 minutes.
- Scald teapot by filling half full with boiling water. Discard water after teapot is warmed.
- Measure one teaspoon of loose tea per cup of tea to be served and one extra teaspoon "for the pot." If using tea bags, use three per standard-sized teapot.
- Pour boiling water over tea leaves and allow to steep for 5 minutes.
- Serve immediately.

Semi-Formal State Dinner Recipes

SESAME-SOY COD

This is a true crowd pleaser. Sometimes I cut the fish into smaller pieces and serve bite-sized pieces as a hot hors d'oeuvre. Many types of fish can be substituted for cod.

1/4 cup orange-juice concentrate
1/2 cup water
1/2 cup catsup
2 Tbsp. soy sauce
1/2 cup cider vinegar
1 Tbsp. sesame oil
1/2 cup brown sugar
1 1/2 lb. cod, cut into 6 pieces, about 1-inch thick
Nonstick cooking spray
1 1/2 Tbsp. sesame seeds, optional

Combine orange-juice concentrate, water, catsup, soy sauce, vinegar, sesame oil, and brown sugar. Set aside. Place fish in a shallow cake pan and pour marinade over fish. Cover and refrigerate for 2 to 3 hours, turning several times and spooning sauce over the top of the fish. Preheat the broiler. Spray the broiler-pan rack with nonstick cooking spray. Broil the fish about 6 inches from the heating element for 4 to 5 minutes on each side. Baste the fish with marinade after turning. If desired, sprinkle fish with sesame seeds. (Children will often prefer the fish without sesame seeds.) *Preparation time = 10 minutes. Marinating time = 3 hours. Broiling time = 10 minutes.*

NUTRITION FACTS—Serving size = 4 oz. • Servings = 6 • Calories = 243 • Total fat = 5 gm. • Cholesterol = 0 mg. • Sodium = 763 mg. • Total carbohydrate = 29 gm. • Dietary fiber = <1 gm. • Protein = 20 gm.

EXCHANGE VALUES—4 lean meat, 1 fat

TWICE-BAKED POTATOES

These are my son's favorite potatoes. Since he began counting fat grams about a year ago, I have lowered the fat in this recipe. He doesn't notice the difference.

>4 medium baking potatoes (Idaho potatoes are best.)
>1/2 cup nonfat sour cream
>1 egg (or 1/4 cup liquid egg substitute)
>2 Tbsp. skim milk
>1/4 tsp. black pepper
>1/4 cup nonfat cheddar cheese, shredded
>Nonstick cooking spray

Preheat oven to 425°. Scrub potatoes and pierce them with a fork. Bake for 45 minutes or until easily squeezed using a pot holder. Allow to cool. Cut potatoes in half lengthwise. Scoop potato pulp out of halves into a bowl, leaving enough potato clinging to the skins so that they can be easily handled without falling apart. Place skins in a cake pan sprayed with nonstick cooking spray. Mix sour cream, egg, milk, and pepper with potato pulp until very smooth and creamy. Place mashed potato mixture into potato shells. Bake covered for 20 to 25 minutes or until lightly browned. Turn off oven. Uncover and sprinkle with cheddar cheese. Bake for 3 to 5 minutes or until cheese melts. *Preparation time = 15 minutes. Baking time = 1 hour and 10 minutes.*

NUTRITION FACTS—Serving size = 1 potato • Servings = 4 • Calories = 198 • Total fat = 2 gm. • Cholesterol (with egg) = 54 mg. • Cholesterol (with egg substitute) = <1 mg. • Sodium = 103 mg. • Total carbohydrate = 39 gm. • Dietary fiber = 3 gm. • Protein = 9 gm.

EXCHANGE VALUES—2 bread/starch, 1/2 fat

CHERRY-COKE SALAD

20-oz. can crushed pineapple, drained
3/4 cup frozen sweet black cherries, save any juice
2 0.3-oz. packages sugar-free cherry gelatin
12 oz. Coca-Cola
1/2 cup walnuts, chopped
6 oz. nonfat cream cheese
Nonstick cooking spray

Combine pineapple and cherry juice, and bring to a boil; add to gelatin. Stir until dissolved. Cool. Add Coca-Cola to cooled gelatin. Chill until slightly thickened. Add drained pineapple, cherries, and 1/4 cup of nuts. Spray a ring mold or 8" x 8" x 2" pan with nonstick cooking spray. Pour mixture into the mold or pan. Chill until firm. Spread cream cheese on top of the firm gelatin. Sprinkle with remaining nuts.

NUTRITION FACTS—Serving size = 1/2 cup • Servings = 10 • Calories = 121 • Total fat = 6 gm. • Cholesterol = 19 mg. • Sodium = 85 mg. • Total carbohydrate = 16 gm. • Dietary fiber = 0 gm. • Protein = 2 gm.

EXCHANGE VALUE—1 bread/starch, 1 fat

FLAMING BANANAS FOSTER

My friend Peg has served this to governors and presidents of universities and always gets the same complimentary response. Feel free to substitute whatever fruit is in season.

>*1/2 cup brown sugar*
>*1/4 cup low-fat margarine*
>*Juice from 1 lemon*
>*Juice from 1 orange*
>*4 bananas, sliced lengthwise in half and then in half again*
>*1/4 cup 150 proof dark rum*
>*4 one-half cup scoops of low-fat frozen yogurt*

Caramelize brown sugar in margarine by heating in a small skillet until margarine appears browned. Add lemon and orange juices. Cook until juice is absorbed. Add bananas. Pour rum over mixture and ignite. DO NOT HEAT RUM AHEAD OF TIME. Spoon over yogurt and serve while still flaming. Note: If you use brandy instead of rum, you need to warm it before igniting. *Preparation time = 15 minutes.*

NUTRITION FACTS—Serving size = 1 banana and 1/2 cup yogurt • Servings = 4 • Calories = 398 • Total fat = 10 gm. • Cholesterol = 10 mg. • Sodium = 286 mg. • Total carbohydrate = 65 gm. • Dietary fiber = 2 gm. • Protein = 8 gm.

EXCHANGE VALUES—2 1/2 bread/starch, 1 fruit, 1/2 skim milk, 2 fat

Oval Office Breakfast Recipes

PRESIDENTIAL FLANNEL CAKES

Many of my friends say these are the best pancakes I have ever served.

> 1 Tbsp. low-fat margarine
> 2 cups flour
> 1/2 tsp. salt
> 4 tsp. baking powder
> 2 eggs or 2 egg whites plus 1/2 cup liquid egg substitute (if you use egg substitute, you will still need to separate 2 eggs in order to whip the egg whites)
> 2 cups skim milk
> Nonstick cooking spray

Rub the margarine into the flour, then add the salt and baking powder. Set aside. Separate the yolks from the whites of the eggs. Beat the egg yolks lightly; add the milk and beat well. Add the milk to the flour mixture, stirring until quite smooth. Beat the whites lightly and fold into the batter. Spoon approximately 1/8 cup for each pancake. Fry until golden brown in heated nonstick pan or griddle sprayed with nonstick cooking spray. Flip once. Note: To test if the griddle is ready, spatter with a few drops of water. If the water spits as it hits, your griddle is ready. *Preparation time = 30 minutes.*

NUTRITION FACTS—Serving size = 1 pancake • Servings = 16 • Calories = 80 • Total fat = 1 gm. • Cholesterol (with egg) – 27 mg. • Cholesterol (with egg substitute) = <1 mg. • Sodium = 158 mg. • Total carbohydrate = 14 gm. • Dietary fiber = <1 gm. • Protein = 3 gm.

EXCHANGE VALUES—1 bread/starch

Cream Tea With the First Lady Recipes

OATMEAL RAISIN SCONES

3/4 cup old-fashioned rolled oats
1 1/2 cups flour
2 tsp. baking powder
1 pkg. Sweet 'N Low sugar substitute
1/4 tsp. salt
1/4 tsp. baking soda
1/3 cup low-fat margarine
1/2 cup raisins or currants
1/3 cup buttermilk
1/3 cup skim milk
Flour for kneading
Nonstick cooking spray
1 1/2 tsp. low-fat margarine, melted

Preheat oven to 400°. Set aside 2 tablespoons of rolled oats. In a large bowl, combine flour, remaining rolled oats, baking powder, Sweet 'N Low, salt, and baking soda. Cut in the margarine using a pastry blender (or two knives) until the mixture resembles coarse crumbs. Stir in raisins or currants. Add the milks to the dry ingredients, and mix lightly with a fork until the mixture clings together and forms a soft dough. Turn dough onto a lightly floured surface and knead gently 5 or 6 times. Divide dough in half. With a lightly floured rolling pin, roll one half of dough into a 7-inch round. Cut into 6 wedges. Repeat process with remaining dough. Place wedges (scones) an inch apart on a baking sheet sprayed with nonstick cooking spray. Pierce tops with tines of fork and brush with melted margarine. Sprinkle with reserved oatmeal and bake for 15 to 18 minutes or until golden brown. Serve warm. *Preparation time = 20 minutes. Baking time = 18 minutes.*

NUTRITION FACTS—Serving size = 1 scone • Servings = 12 • Calories = 106 • Total fat = 1 gm. • Cholesterol = <1 mg. • Sodium = 126 mg. • Total carbohydrate = 22 gm. • Dietary fiber = 1 gm. • Protein = 3 gm.

EXCHANGE VALUES—1 bread/starch, 1/2 fruit

CARROT SANDWICHES

2 cups carrots, chopped
1/2 cup onion, chopped
1/4 cup low-fat mayonnaise
1/4 cup low-fat cream cheese (or Neufchatel cheese)
1/2 tsp. Beau Monde seasoning
4 tsp. dill weed
1 tsp. Mrs. Dash salt-free seasoning
12 slices whole wheat bread
6 lettuce leaves
Red radish peel (for garnish)

Place 1/2 cup water in a blender. Gradually add carrots, and chop. Drain well, and set aside. Place 1/4 cup water in blender. Add onion. Chop, then drain and set aside. Blend mayonnaise, cream cheese, carrots, and onions. Add seasonings. Refrigerate for an hour. Trim crusts from bread. Use 1/3 to 1/2 cup of filling for 2 slices of bread. Add a lettuce leaf to each sandwich and cut into quarters. Garnish with radish peel. *Preparation time = 15 minutes. Refrigeration time = 1 hour.*

NUTRITION FACTS—Serving size = 1/4th of a sandwich • Servings = 24 • Calories = 51 • Total fat = 4 gm. • Cholesterol = 6 mg. • Sodium = 191 mg. • Total carbohydrate = 8 gm. • Dietary fiber = 3 gm. • Protein = 2 gm.

EXCHANGE VALUES—1/2 bread/starch, 1/2 fat

MAMIE EISENHOWER FUDGE

This recipe is shared by my dear friend, Annie Blocker. She and her husband, Dave, plan to start a bed and breakfast in Iowa.

> 4 1/2 cups sugar
> 1/4 tsp. salt
> 2 Tbsp. low-fat margarine
> 12-oz. can evaporated milk
> 12 oz. sweet German chocolate
> 12 oz. semi-sweet chocolate chips
> 1 pint marshmallow creme
> 2 cups walnut meats
> Nonfat cooking spray

Combine sugar, salt, margarine, and evaporated milk in a large saucepan. Bring to a rolling boil for 6 minutes. Combine the next four ingredients in a large mixing bowl. Add chocolate mixture to sugar mixture, and beat until chocolate is thoroughly melted and candy is smooth. Spray a 9" x 13" cake pan with nonfat cooking spray. Place fudge in pan and let stand until cool and set. *Preparation time = 15 minutes.*

NUTRITION FACTS—Serving size = 1 piece • Servings = 40 • Calories = 285 • Total fat = 12 gm. • Cholesterol = 2 mg. • Sodium = 37 mg. • Total carbohydrates = 44 gm. • Dietary fiber = <1 gm. • Protein = 3 gm.

EXCHANGE VALUES—2 1/2 bread/starch, 2 fat.

NOTE: THIS RECIPE IS NOT SUITABLE FOR MOST INDIVIDUALS FOLLOWING A DIET LOW IN SIMPLE SUGARS.

FRANNIE'S MAIDS OF HONOR

Frannie Blum arrives at the Parson's Inn with her own sweets to share—something she was taught to make as a child. She calls them her Maids of Honor.

> *1/4 cup low-fat margarine*
> *1/2 cup sugar*
> *1 tsp. vanilla*
> *2 eggs (or 1/2 cup liquid egg substitute)*
> *1 tsp. baking powder*
> *1 tsp. baking soda*
> *1 3/4 cup flour*
> *1/2 cup fruit spread of your choice*

Preheat oven to 325°. Cream margarine, sugar, and vanilla in a mixing bowl. Add beaten eggs, one at a time. Add dry ingredients, mixing well. Press about 1 tablespoon of dough into mini-muffin tins to form a shell. Fill with favorite fruit spread, using about 1 heaping teaspoon of fruit for each. Bake for 15 minutes. *Preparation time = 15 minutes. Baking time = 15 minutes.*

NUTRITION FACTS—Serving size = 1 piece • Servings = 24 • Calories = 63 • Total fat = 2 gm. • Cholesterol (with egg) = 18 mg. • Cholesterol (with egg substitute) = 0 mg. • Sodium = 95 mg. • Total carbohydrate = 11 gm. • Dietary fiber = <1 gm. • Protein = 1 gm.

EXCHANGE VALUES—1/2 bread/starch, 1/2 fat

White House Dining Shopping List

Take this book along to your supermarket or photocopy the list. Select the same number or size of items that you have in the past, based on the number of people for whom you are shopping. Review this list before you go to the store. Cross out items you have on hand, and write in your personal likes and needs.

Produce

Potatoes
Carrots
Onions
Leaf lettuce
Red radishes
Lemons
Orange
Bananas

Packaged

Raisins or currants
Sugar-free cherry gelatin
Walnuts
Coffee
Rolled oats
Apricot herbal tea
Sweet German Chocolate
Semi-sweet chocolate bits
Sweet 'N Low
Sugar cubes
Tea

Staples/Spices

Flour
Salt
Brown sugar
Beau Monde seasoning
Pepper
Baking powder
Baking soda
Sugar
Vanilla
Sesame seeds
Mrs. Dash
Dill weed
Sesame Oil

Bottled/Canned

Crushed pineapple
Low-fat mayonnaise
Catsup
Maple syrup
Soy sauce
Cider vinegar
Evaporated milk
Marshmallow creme
Fruit spread

Frozen Case

Orange juice
Sweet black cherries
Low-fat whipped topping
Low-fat frozen yogurt

Refrigerator Case

Skim milk
Cream or cream substitute
Low-fat cream cheese
Low-fat margarine
Eggs or egg substitute
Buttermilk
Nonfat sour cream
Nonfat cheddar cheese
Butter

Meat Case

Cod, fresh or frozen

Bakery/Deli

Whole wheat dinner rolls
Whole wheat bread

Snack Foods

Coca-Cola

Other

Asti Spumante
   non-alcoholic champagne
150 proof dark rum
Nonstick cooking spray

COMPANY'S COMING

GRANDMA & GRANDPA'S VISIT
•
BEST FRIENDS ARRIVE

Grandma and Grandpa's Visit

All the plans are in place, every room is neat as a pin, and everyone's excited for the visitors to arrive. Not much longer and they'll be here!

It's only once a year that Grandma and Grandpa come to visit. All the preparation, all the straightening, all the fuss—everyone wants them to have fun while they're in town.

The week before they arrive, we usually spend an hour brainstorming menus that our guests may like (we also include our own favorites). When Grandpa talked about the cream puffs he ate as a child, we planned a meal to include them.

If you're uncertain what Grandma and Grandpa's likes and dislikes are, do a little investigative work during this visit. Suggest they send you their favorite recipes to add to your collection. Practice making these during the year and have them ready as a surprise at the next visit.

Grandma and Grandpa's Visit Activities

1. Make a master list of all chores that need to be done before Grandma and Grandpa come.

2. Review and practice basic manners that will make the visit go smoothly.

3. Make journal notes of interesting conversations, especially about your grandparents' history and life experiences. Writing these down can be an enjoyable and invaluable way to capture their past, and to pass down information to future generations.

4. Work on updating the family tree with your grandparents; they may be flattered by your interest.

GRANDMA AND GRANDPA'S VISIT MENUS

LET GRANDMA HELP BREAKFAST

* Buttermilk Pancakes
    Warmed Low-Calorie Syrup
    Orange Juice

Skim Milk
Coffee

AFTER CHURCH BRUNCH

* Tropical Ham Slices
    Fresh Melon
* Parson's Inn Sweet Rolls

* Parson's Inn Caramel Rolls
    Skim Milk
    Grape Juice

STORY TELLING SUPPER

* Old-Fashioned Crockpot Stew
    Rice
* Carrot Lentil Salad
    Dinner Rolls

* Banana Cake
    Skim Milk
    Coffee or Tea

(* recipe follows)

Let Grandma Help Breakfast Recipes

BUTTERMILK PANCAKES

1 1/4 cup flour
2 Tbsp. sugar
1 tsp. baking powder
1/2 tsp. baking soda
1/8 tsp. salt
1 beaten egg (or 1/4 cup liquid egg substitute)
1 1/3 cup buttermilk
2 tsp. canola oil
Nonstick cooking spray

In a mixing bowl, stir together flour, sugar, baking powder, baking soda, and salt. Set aside. Combine egg, buttermilk, and oil; add liquid ingredients all at once to flour mixture, then stir until blended but still slightly lumpy. Pour about 1/4 cup batter onto hot griddle sprayed with nonstick cooking spray. Cook until golden brown, turning to cook other side when pancakes have a bubbly surface and slightly dry edges. Note: You may have to add additional buttermilk to thin the batter. Just remember, this batter is supposed to be rather thick. *Preparation time = 30 minutes.*

NUTRITION FACTS—Serving size = 2 4-inch pancakes • Servings = 5 • Calories = 190 • Total fat = 4 gm. • Cholesterol (with egg) = 45 mg. • Cholesterol (with egg substitute) = 2 mg. • Sodium = 358 mg. • Total carbohydrate = 32 gm. • Dietary fiber = <1 gm. • Protein = 7 gm.

EXCHANGE VALUES—2 bread/starch, 1 fat

After Church Brunch Recipes

TROPICAL HAM SLICES

1/2 cup dried apricots
3/4 cup water
1 cup crushed pineapple with juice
1/4 cup brown sugar
1 tsp. prepared mustard
1/2 tsp. nutmeg
1/2 tsp. garlic powder
4 3-oz. slices 93% fat-free ham, sliced 3/4-inch thick
Nonstick cooking spray

Preheat oven to 350°. Spray casserole dish with nonstick cooking spray. Cook apricots with water for 5 minutes; drain, saving liquid. Add pineapple with juice, brown sugar, mustard, and spices to apricots, and cook for about 5 minutes. Layer ham in casserole dish and pour fruit mixture over it. Bake covered for 30 minutes. *Preparation time = 15 minutes. Baking time = 30 minutes.*

NUTRITION FACTS—Serving size = 1 slice • Servings = 4 • Calories = 221 • Total fat = 4 gm. • Cholesterol = 39 mg. • Sodium = 1,104 mg. • Total carbohydrate = 30 mg. • Dietary fiber = 0 gm. • Protein = 17 gm.

EXCHANGE VALUES—2 lean meat, 1 1/2 bread/starch

PARSON'S INN SWEET ROLLS

2 pkgs. dry yeast or 1 heaping Tbsp. bulk yeast
1 Tbsp. sugar
1 cup lukewarm water
1 cup skim milk
6 Tbsp. low-fat margarine
1/2 cup sugar
1 tsp. salt
3 eggs, beaten (or 3/4 cup liquid egg substitute)
6 1/2 cups flour
1/4 to 1/2 cup flour (for kneading)
3 Tbsp. low-fat margarine
2 tsp. cinnamon
1/2 cup brown sugar

Dissolve yeast and 1 tablespoon sugar in lukewarm water. Let stand for at least 15 minutes. Meanwhile, warm milk and 6 tablespoons margarine in microwave. Add sugar, salt, and beaten eggs. Pour mixture into a large bowl, and add yeast mixture. Add flour, 2 cups at a time—mixing between additions. After last flour is added, knead to a soft dough consistency and form into a ball. (Sprinkle a little flour under and around the dough to help with kneading. Also, spray your hands with nonstick cooking spray before kneading to avoid sticking.)

Cover with a clean towel and let rise in a warm area. Allow dough to rise three times, punching down and kneading dough 10 to 15 times and turning dough every 5 times. Dough is ready to knead when doubled in size. After the third time, divide dough in half. Place dough on floured board and roll out to a 12" x 14" rectangle. Spread on rectangle a mixture of 3 tablespoons margarine, 2 teaspoons cinnamon, and 1/2 cup brown sugar. Roll dough tightly and cut into 3/4- to 1-inch wheels. Spray a 9" x 12" cake pan with nonstick cooking spray.

Place dough wheels in pan. Let rise about 45 minutes or until dough almost doubles. Preheat oven to 350°. Bake for 12 to 15 minutes or until lightly browned. Cover rolls with foil to keep them moist. After cooling, spread with frosting and serve.

NUTRITION FACTS—Serving size = 1 roll • Servings = 36 • Calories = 155 • Total fat = 3 gm. • Cholesterol (with egg) = 18 mg. • Cholesterol (with egg substitute) = <1 mg. • Sodium = 109 mg. • Total carbohydrate = 26 gm. • Dietary fiber = <1 gm. • Protein = 3 gm.

EXCHANGE VALUES—1 1/2 bread/starch, 1/2 fat

PARSON'S INN CARAMEL ROLLS

2 pkgs. dry yeast or 1 heaping Tbsp. bulk yeast
1 Tbsp. sugar
1 cup lukewarm water
1 cup skim milk
6 Tbsp. low-fat margarine
1/2 cup sugar
1 tsp. salt
3 eggs, beaten (or 3/4 cup liquid egg substitute)
6 1/2 cups flour
1/4 to 1/2 cup flour (for kneading)
3 Tbsp. low-fat margarine
2 tsp. cinnamon
1/2 cup brown sugar

CARAMEL MIXTURE FOR BOTTOM OF PAN:

6 Tbsp. low-fat margarine
1/3 cup brown sugar
3/4 cup pecans (whole or broken)

Dissolve yeast and 1 tablespoon sugar in lukewarm water. Let stand for at least 15 minutes. Meanwhile, warm milk and 6 tablespoons margarine in microwave. Add sugar, salt, and beaten eggs.

Pour mixture into a large bowl, and add yeast mixture. Add flour, 2 cups at a time—mixing between additions. After last flour is added, knead to a soft dough consistency and form into a ball. (Sprinkle a little flour under and around the dough to help with kneading. Also, spray your hands with nonstick cooking spray before kneading to avoid sticking.)

Cover with a clean towel and let rise in a warm area. Allow dough to rise three times, punching down and kneading dough 10 to 15 times and turning dough every 5 times. Dough is ready to knead when doubled in size. After the third time, divide dough in half. Place dough on floured board and roll out to a 12" x 14" rectangle. Spread on rectangle a mixture of 3 tablespoons margarine, 2 teaspoons cinnamon, and 1/2 cup brown sugar. Roll dough tightly and cut into 3/4- to 1-inch wheels. Spray a 9" x 12" cake pan with nonstick cooking spray.

Preheat oven to 350°. Combine 6 tablespoons margarine, 1/3 cup brown sugar, and 3/4 cup whole or broken pecans. Place in microwave until margarine is melted. Pour in bottom of cake pan, spreading evenly. Place dough wheels on top of nut mixture, and bake for 12 to 15 minutes or until lightly browned. To remove, invert pan over a large tray covered with aluminum foil. Leave for 5 to 10 minutes. Pan will lift off and pecan rolls will be bottom side up.

NUTRITION FACTS—Serving size =1 roll • Servings = 36 • Calories = 202 • Total fat = 7 gm. • Cholesterol (with egg) = 6 mg. • Cholesterol (with egg substitute) = <1 mg. • Sodium = 121 mg. • Total carbohydrate = 28 gm. • Dietary fiber = 1 gm. • Protein = 4 gm.

EXCHANGE VALUES—2 bread/starch, 1 1/2 fat

Story Telling Supper Recipes

OLD-FASHIONED CROCKPOT STEW

> 2 lb. stew meat
> 1/2 cup dry red wine
> 4 oz. whole fresh mushrooms
> 15 3/4-oz. can Healthy Choice cream of mushroom soup
> 1 package onion soup mix

Mix all ingredients together in a Crockpot. Cook on low for 8 to 10 hours or on high heat for 3 to 4 hours. If you wish, this may be served over noodles or rice. *Preparation time = 15 minutes. Cooking time = 3 to 10 hours.*

NUTRITION FACTS—Serving size = 1 cup • Servings = 10 • Calories = 291 • Total fat = 13 gm. • Cholesterol = 89 mg. • Sodium = 524 mg. • Total carbohydrate = 5 gm. • Dietary fiber = <1 gm. • Protein = 27

EXCHANGE VALUES—4 medium-fat meat

CARROT LENTIL SALAD

Diane Barton adapted this recipe from one featured in Country Magazine. *The original author was Monica Wilcott of Sturgis, Saskatchewan.*

> 1 cup dry lentils
> 1 1/2 cup diced carrots
> 1 bay leaf
> 2 garlic cloves, minced
> 2 Tbsp. dried celery flakes
> 1/4 cup finely chopped fresh or 1 Tbsp. dried parsley
> 2 Tbsp. olive oil
> 1/4 cup lemon juice
> 1/2 tsp. salt
> 1/2 tsp. dried thyme
> 1/4 tsp. pepper

In a casserole dish, combine lentils, carrots, and bay leaf. Cover with an inch of water. Bring to a boil, then simmer for 15 to 20 minutes or until lentils are tender. Remove bay leaf; drain, and cool. To make dressing, combine remaining ingredients. Pour over lentil mixture. Cover and refrigerate several hours. *Preparation time = 30 minutes. Refrigeration time = 3 hours.*

NUTRITION FACTS—Serving size = 3/4 cup • Servings = 6 • Calories = 184 • Total fat = 5 gm. • Cholesterol = 0 mg. • Sodium = 223 mg. • Total carbohydrate = 27 gm. • Dietary fiber = 3 gm. • Protein = 10 gm.

EXCHANGE VALUES—1 1/2 bread/starch, 1 vegetable, 1 fat

BANANA CAKE

1/2 cup low-fat margarine
1/2 cup sugar
2 eggs (or 1/2 cup liquid egg substitute)
1 Tbsp. liquid Sweet 'N Low
1/2 cup buttermilk
1 tsp. vanilla
2 cups flour
1/2 tsp. salt
1 tsp. baking soda
1 tsp. baking powder
1 1/2 cups mashed ripe bananas
  (about 2 large bananas)
Nonstick cooking spray
Low-calorie whipped topping
Fresh mint (for garnish)

Preheat oven to 350°. Cream margarine and sugar, then add eggs, Sweet 'N Low, buttermilk, and vanilla. Set aside. In another bowl, combine dry ingredients. Add the dry ingredients, mixing well. Fold in mashed bananas last. Pour batter into two 8-inch bread pans sprayed with nonstick cooking spray. Bake for 25 to 30 minutes.

OPTIONAL: To serve, layer cake, thinly sliced bananas, and low-calorie whipped topping; place a dollop of whipped topping on top of each slice and garnish with sprig of mint or any other green herb. *Preparation time = 10 minutes. Baking time = 30 minutes.*

NUTRITION FACTS—Serving size = 1/20th of cake • Servings = 20 • Calories = 113 • Total fat = 3 gm. • Cholesterol (with egg) = 25 mg. • Cholesterol (with egg substitute) = 3 mg. • Sodium = 148 mg. • Total carbohydrate = 20 gm. • Dietary fiber = <1 gm. • Protein = 2 gm.

EXCHANGE VALUES—1 bread/starch, 1/2 fat

Grandma and Grandpa's Visit Shopping List

Take this book along to your supermarket or photocopy the list. Select the same number or size of items that you have in the past, based on the number of people for whom you are shopping. Review this list before you go to the store. Cross out items you have on hand, and write in your personal likes and needs.

Produce

Celery
Parsley
Carrots
Garlic
Mushrooms
Melons
Bananas

Packaged

Pecans
Liquid Sweet 'N Low
Dry lentils
Onion soup mix
Yeast
Coffee
Dried apricots
Rice
Tea

Staples/Spices

Brown sugar
Nutmeg
Garlic powder
Sugar
Flour
Parsley
Celery leaves
Bay leaf
Olive oil
Canola oil
Salt
Thyme
Baking soda
Baking powder
Vanilla
Pepper
Cinnamon

Bottled/Canned

Low-calorie maple-flavored
   syrup
Crushed pineapple
Grape juice
Lemon juice
Healthy Choice cream
   of mushroom soup
Prepared mustard

Frozen Case

Low-calorie whipped topping
Orange juice

Refrigerated Case

Low-fat margarine
Eggs or egg substitute
Buttermilk
Skim milk

Meat Case

Ham (93% fat free)
Stew meat

Bakery/Deli

Dinner rolls

Other

Dry red wine
Nonstick cooking spray

BEST FRIENDS ARRIVE

The park on Friday, downtown shopping on Saturday, and a delicious brunch by the fire on Sunday. You've thought about how to keep your weekend busy while saving enough time for spontaneity. It will all come together once they arrive!

It's not every day your best friends come to visit. Whether it's been a long time since you've seen each other or just last year, it's an exciting time.

Before they arrive, it may be helpful to make a list of everyone's favorite foods. Shop ahead for nonperishable ingredients, and keep a special shelf in your pantry and freezer for these items.

The recipes in this section are simple and delicious. However you spend your weekend, have fun and enjoy!

BEST FRIENDS ARRIVE ACTIVITIES

1. Prepare for your friends' arrival by organizing a family shopping trip to stock the pantry. You may want to keep these foods on hand:

   Whole-grain breads, rolls, and crackers
   Low-sodium broth or bouillon
   Low-fat cheese
   Cornstarch
   Cream of mushroom soup
   Eggs or egg substitute
   Flour
   Fruit, frozen or canned
   Garlic
   Lemon juice
   Dry lentils
   Margarine

Canned mushrooms
Nonfat dried milk
Noodles and pastas
Olive oil
Onions
Pancake mix
Pizza dough
Rice
Low-sodium soy sauce
Variety of spices and seasonings
Sugar
Canned tomatoes
Tomato sauce or tomato puree
Tuna
Vegetables, frozen or canned
Vegetable oil
Water chestnuts
Worcestershire sauce

2. Share old letters, yearbooks, mementos, and items held dear with best friends and their families.

3. Play your favorite old music and get everybody dancing. Recent studies suggest that life's little pleasures, such as dancing with your children, may give a boost to your immune system.

Best Friends Arrive Menus

Raid the Pantry Dinner

* Turkey Stroganoff
  Whole Wheat Noodles
  French-Style Green Beans
  Frozen Vanilla Yogurt With
  Chocolate Topping

Potato Rolls
* Applesauce Date Cookies
Skim Milk
Coffee or Tea

Sleep-In Sunday Morning Brunch

* Parson's Inn Overnight Egg Bake
* Fresh Fruit Platter
  Twelve-Grain Toast

Orange Juice
Skim Milk
Coffee or Tea

Story Telling Supper

* Salsa Hamburger
* Chili and Cheddar Buns
  Canned Pears With Maraschino Cherries

* Picante Vegetables
Pumpernickel Bread
Skim Milk

(* recipe follows)

Raid the Pantry Dinner Recipes

TURKEY STROGANOFF

1/2 cup minced onion
1 tsp. crushed garlic
1 Tbsp. olive oil
1 lb. ground turkey
2 Tbsp. flour
1/4 tsp. salt
1/4 tsp. pepper
1 lb. fresh mushrooms, sliced or
  8-oz. can sliced mushrooms, drained
10 1/2-oz. can low-fat, low-sodium
  cream of chicken soup
1/2 cup nonfat sour cream
Parsley

Sauté onion and garlic in olive oil over medium heat. Stir in turkey, and brown. Stir in flour, salt, pepper, and mushrooms. Cook 5 minutes. Stir in soup; simmer uncovered 10 minutes. Serve with rice or noodles and sour cream. Garnish with parsley. *Preparation time = 30 minutes.*

NUTRITION FACTS—Serving size = 3/4 cup • Servings = 6 • Calories = 280 • Total fat = 14 gm. • Cholesterol = 82 mg. • Sodium = 389 mg. • Total carbohydrate = 14 gm. • Dietary fiber = 2 gm. • Protein = 25 gm.

EXCHANGE VALUES   3 lean meat, 1 bread/starch, 1 fat (without noodles)

APPLESAUCE DATE COOKIES

1/4 cup canola oil
1/4 cup sugar
1 egg (or 1/4 cup liquid egg substitute)
1 tsp. vanilla extract
1/2 cup unsweetened applesauce
1/2 cup whole wheat flour
1/2 cup unbleached white flour
2 tsp. baking powder
1/2 tsp. baking soda
1 tsp. cinnamon
1/4 tsp. allspice
1/2 cup rolled oats
1/2 cup dates, chopped fine
Nonstick cooking spray

Preheat oven to 375°. Cream the oil and sugar together. Add the egg, and beat until light. Blend in the vanilla and applesauce. Stir the remaining ingredients into the creamed mixture. Blend well. Drop by teaspoonfuls onto a baking sheet sprayed lightly with nonstick cooking spray. Bake for 10 minutes. Cool on a wire rack. Makes 2 dozen cookies. (Note: Raisins can be used instead of dates.) *Preparation time = 15 minutes. Baking time = 10 minutes.*

NUTRITION FACTS—Serving size = 1 cookie • Servings = 24 • Calories = 66 • Total fat = <1 gm. • Cholesterol (with egg) = 9 mg. • Cholesterol (with egg substitute) = 0 mg. • Sodium =70 mg. • Total carbohydrate = 10 gm. • Dietary fiber = <1 gm. • Protein = 1 gm.

EXCHANGE VALUES—1 bread/starch

Sleep-In Brunch Recipes

PARSON'S INN OVERNIGHT EGG BAKE

This should be prepared the night before and refrigerated until baking.

> 8 slices whole wheat bread, cubed
> 2 lbs. (4 cups) turkey ham, cut into 1/2" cubes
> 2 10-oz. packages frozen chopped broccoli
> 2 4-oz. cans mushroom pieces and stems
> 6 eggs (or 1 1/2 cups liquid egg substitute)
> 1 1/2 tsp. garlic powder
> 1 1/2 tsp. onion powder
> 3 cups skim milk
> 4 Tbsp. flour
> 2 Tbsp. prepared mustard
> 8-oz. package fat-free grated mozzarella cheese
> *Nonstick cooking spray*

Preheat oven to 375°. Spray a 9" x 13" cake pan with nonstick cooking spray. Layer bread cubes, ham, broccoli, and mushrooms in pan. Set aside. Mix eggs, garlic powder, onion powder, milk, flour, and mustard. Pour over layers in cake pan. Sprinkle cheese on top. Bake for 40 to 50 minutes covered; uncover and bake for 10 minutes more. Remove from oven and allow to set up for 5 to 10 minutes before serving. Place on spinach leaves or any other greens on large platter. (I garnish with cherry tomatoes in the summer and sprigs of grapes in the winter.) *Preparation time = 15 minutes. Baking time = 1 hour.*

NUTRITION FACTS—Serving size = 1/16 recipe • Servings = 16 • Calories = 186 • Total fat = 6 gm. • Cholesterol (with egg) = 81 mg. • Cholesterol (with egg substitute) = <1 mg. • Sodium = 766 mg. • Total carbohydrate = 14 gm. • Dietary fiber = 1 gm. • Protein = 20 gm.

EXCHANGE VALUES—1/2 bread/starch, 1/2 skim milk, 1 lean meat, 1/2 vegetable, 1 fat

FRESH FRUIT PLATTER

Lettuce or spinach (for garnish)
1 lb. green grapes
2 bananas
1/2 honeydew melon
2 Rome apples

Choose an unusual plate or platter. Place lettuce or spinach leaves around edge to form an attractive border. Wash, peel, chunk, and slice, as desired, the rest of the fruit. You may want to provide a flower effect with one fruit placed in a small dish or fluted bowl in the center of the platter. This works especially well if you have a fruit dip or are offering applesauce. *Preparation time = 15 to 30 minutes.*

NUTRITION FACTS—Serving size = 1 cup • Servings = 6 • Calories = 101 • Total fat = <1 gm. • Cholesterol = 0 mg. • Sodium = 2 mg. • Total carbohydrate = 26 gm. • Dietary fiber = 2 gm. • Protein = 1 gm.

EXCHANGE VALUES—1 1/2 fruit

Story Telling Supper Recipes

SALSA HAMBURGER

1 cup chopped onion
2 lbs. 93% fat-free hamburger
16-oz. can baked beans
1 can no-salt stewed tomatoes
8-oz. jar mild salsa

Brown hamburger and chopped onions in a skillet. Pour off grease as it accumulates. Place in colander and drain well. Place hamburger and onion mixture in a 4-quart saucepan. Add baked beans, stewed tomatoes, and mild salsa. Reheat thoroughly on medium heat, about 10 minutes, stirring occasionally. Preparation time = 20 minutes.

NUTRITION FACTS—Serving size = 1/2 cup • Servings per recipe = 16 • Calories = 188 • Total fat = 9 gm. • Cholesterol = 53 mg. • Sodium = 261 mg. • Total carbohydrate = 7 gm. • Dietary fiber = <1 gm. • Protein = 17 gm.

EXCHANGE VALUES—2 medium-fat meat, 1/2 vegetable, 1/2 fat

CHILI AND CHEDDAR BUNS

1 tube refrigerated buttermilk biscuit dough
1/2 cup shredded reduced-fat cheddar cheese
2 Tbsp. chopped green chilies
Nonstick cooking spray

Preheat oven to 400°. Remove biscuits from tube. Use a kitchen scissors to cut biscuits into 6 to 8 chunks. Spray an 8-inch square baking pan with non-stick cooking spray. Mix pieces of dough with cheese and chilies in the pan. Bake for 8 to 10 minutes, until golden brown. Break buns apart and serve warm. *Preparation time = 5 minutes. Baking time = 10 minutes.*

NUTRITION FACTS—Serving size = 1 bun • Servings = 8 • Calories = 113 • Total fat = 5 gm. • Cholesterol = 8 mg. • Sodium = 430 mg. • Total carbohydrate = 13 gm. • Dietary fiber = <1 gm. • Protein = 4 gm.

EXCHANGE VALUES—1 bread/starch, 1 fat

PICANTE VEGETABLES

2 cups fresh or frozen corn
2 carrots, sliced (about 1 cup)
1/2 cup chopped onion
1/2 cup chopped green pepper
1 cup water
1/2 cup Santa Fe-style medium salsa

Combine all ingredients except salsa in a saucepan. Cook about 10 minutes or until tender. Add salsa just before serving. Rewarm for 5 minutes. Preparation time = 20 minutes.

NUTRITION FACTS—Serving size = 1/2 cup • Servings = 6 • Calories = 100 • Total fat = 0 gm. • Cholesterol = 0 mg. • Sodium = 213 mg.• Total carbohydrate = 25 gm. • Dietary fiber = 1 gm. • Protein = 3 gm.

EXCHANGE VALUES—1 bread/starch, 1 vegetable

Best Friends Arrive Shopping List

Take this book along to your supermarket or photocopy the list. Select the same number or size of items that you have in the past, based on the number of people for whom you are shopping. Review this list before you go to the store. Cross out items you have on hand, and write in your personal likes and needs.

Produce

Corn
Onions
Garlic
Mushrooms
Parsley
Carrots
Green pepper
Honeydew melon
Muskmelon
Bananas
Green grapes
Lettuce or spinach
Rome apples

Packaged

Whole wheat noodles
Rolled oats
Dates
Coffee
Tea

Staples/Spices

Olive oil
Flour
Salt
Pepper
Canola oil
Sugar
Vanilla
Whole wheat flour
Baking powder
Baking soda
Cinnamon
Allspice
Garlic powder
Onion powder

Bottled/Canned

Prepared mustard
Unsweetened applesauce
Green chilies
Medium salsa
Mild salsa
French-style green beans
Chocolate ice cream topping
Pears
Maraschino cherries
Mushrooms
Low-fat cream of chicken soup
Baked beans
No-salt stewed tomatoes

FROZEN CASE

Frozen vanilla yogurt
Orange juice
Chopped broccoli

REFRIGERATOR CASE

Nonfat sour cream
Eggs or egg substitute
Buttermilk biscuit dough
Reduced-fat cheddar cheese
Skim milk
Fat-free mozzarella cheese

MEAT CASE

Ground turkey
Hamburger
Turkey ham

BAKERY/DELI

Potato rolls
Twelve-grain bread
Pumpernickel bread
Whole wheat bread

OTHER

Nonstick cooking spray

INDEX

Aching muscles lunch, 177
After-church brunch, 41
All day baseball lunch, 159
Almond lemon cookies, 127
Almondine, orange chicken salad, 103
American Indian stew, 217
Angel hair, shrimp and, 18
Annie's fruit dip, 59
Apple bars, 194
Apple bran oven pancake, 212
Apple cardamom bread, 7
Apple cups, 147
Apple raisin compote, 72
Applesauce
  date cookies, 284
  red hot cinnamon, 50
  with dumplings, 167
Asparagus-potato soup, 136
Autumn apple bars, 194
Avocado pita-witch, 69

Back to school, 189
Baked potato melts, 177
Baking powder biscuits, 164
Banana cake, 277
Banana pepper and cucumber salad, 174
Banana-kiwi malt, 32
Bananas Foster, flaming, 258
Bars, apple, 194
Baseball lunch, 159
BBQ sauce, all-purpose, 226
Beach, relaxing at, 113
Bean, hamburger, cookout, 159

Beans, garlic, 166, green, dilly, 225
Best friends arrive, 280
Birthday bash activities, 28
Birthday party celebration recipes, 32
Biscuits, baking powder, 164
BLT pizza, 125
Blueberries, sugared, 39
Board game, recipes, 23
Bottom of ninth grand slam activities, 157
Bran muffins, pumpkin, 203
Bran, apple pancake, 212
Bread
  apple cardamom, 7
  corn, green chilies, 205
  dill cheese, 75
  garlic, 84
  raisin wheat, 176
Breakfast
  at dawn, 184
  at noon, 137
  birder's, 241
  cheerleading, 146
  Halloween, 71
  hurry and dress, 191
  in bed, 39
  let grandma help, 270
  lovers' patio, 49
  make a list, 212
  Oval Office, 259
  pizza, 131
  pregame, 7
  read the rules, 176
  sandwich, Hawaiian, 131
  snow drift, 21
  take your time, 195

Breasts, chicken, tangy, 23
Broccoli and rice casserole, 235
  soup, 63
Brownies, rock star, 110
Brunch
  after church, 271
  holiday, 82
  New Year's, 61
  Oscar day, 102
  recipes, 41
Brunch-style potato pancakes, 137
Buns, chili and cheddar, 288
Buttermilk pancakes, 270

Cabbage and raisin stew, 204
Cabbage potato soup, 192
Caesar's chicken salad, 138
Cake
  banana, 277
  coffee, 32
  Diane's crazy, 215
  New Year's resolutions, 64
  pound, chocolate zucchini, 140
Cakes, flannel, 259
Caramel rolls, Parson's Inn, 273
Cardamom, apple, bread, 7
Cards, pizza and, 123
Carol's peppercorn salad, 13
Carrot
  lentil salad, 276
  sandwiches, 261
  soup, 162
Casserole
  broccoli and rice, 235
  kohlrabi, 243

  mushroom turkey, 165
Celebrate habitat picnic, 243
Celery sauce, vegetable frittata with, 193
Cheddar and chili buns, 288
Cheerleading breakfast recipes, 146
Cheese
  and pea salad, 19
  bread, dill, 75
  potatoes, microwave, 139
  orange dressing, 95
Cheesecake pie, 22
Cheesy potato soup, 8
Cherry-Coke salad, 257
Chestnuts roasting activities, 79
Chicken
  breasts, tangy, 23
  fajita pizza, 128
  lasagna, herbal spinach, 82
  Mexicali, 40
  salad, Caesar's, 138
  salad, orange, almondine, 103
  with Italian pasta, 30
Chili and cheddar buns, 288
Chilies, green, corn bread, 205
Chocolate
  chip cookies, 20
  peanut butter pudding, 130
  sandwiches, 119
  zucchini pound cake, 140
Chops, pork, chutney-style, 201, Italian, 233
Christmas cookie exchange, 85
Chutney, raspberry, Cornish hens with, 172
Chutney-style pork chops, 201
Cilantro eggs, 33

Cindy and Patti's Green Bay
  potatoes, 202
Cinnamon applesauce, 50
Cinnamon-basil nectarine
  pie, 31
Coco-Cola cherry
  salad, 257
Cod, sesame-soy, 255
Coffee, cake, fruity,
Compote, apple raisin, 72,
  fruit, frozen, 191
Cookies
  applesauce date, 284
  chocolate chip, 20
  Christmas, 85
  gingerbread, 86
  Heath-bit, 175
  lemon almond, 127
  peanut butter, 11
  thumbprint, 87
Cooking chart for turkey, 90
Cookout kickoff, 226
Cookout, hamburger bean, 159
Corn bread, green chilies, 205
Corn on the cob, Parmesan
  topped, 116
Cornish hens with raspberry
  chutney, 172
County fair, 199
Cranberry salad, 94
Cream tea etiquette, 253, with
  First Lady, 260
Creamy cucumber soup, 102
Crockpot fruit soup, 185
Crockpot stew, old-fashioned,
  275
Crunchy French toast, 195
Crust, pizza, 10

Cucumber
  and banana pepper, 174
  mint, shrimp sandwiches, 42
  salad, 129
  soup, 102
  spice, 160
  turkey pita pockets, 117
Curled up with a book, 136

Danish frosting, 216
Date cookies, applesauce, 284
Dessert, strawberry Jello, 178
Diane's crazy cake, 215
Dill cheese bread, 75
Dilly green beans, 225
Dinner for two, 47
Dip, fruit, 59, orange burst, 107
Dressing, orange-cheese, 95,
  sage, 91
Dumplings with applesauce,
  167

Easy veggie pizza, 9
Ecology experience, 238
Egg bake, overnight, 285
Eggnog, 88
Eggplant fiesta, 104
Eggs, cilantro, 33
Eisenhower fudge, 262
Eskimo pie, activities, 16

Fajita pizza, chicken, 128
Fall, tailgate, 2
Family vacation, planning, 231
Father's or Mother's Day, 37
First Lady, cream tea with, 260
Fish, red pepper, 5
Flaming bananas Foster, 258

INDEX

Flannel cakes, presidential, 259
Football heroes smorgasbord, 151
Frannie's maids of honor, 263
French toast, 49, 195
  pecan-stuffed, 146
Fresh fruit platter, 286
Frittata, vegetable, 193
Frosting, Danish, 216
Fruit
  compote, frozen, 191
  dip, Annie's, 59, orange burst, 107
  fresh platter, 286
  pizza, 126
  plate, movie star, 106
  portrait of, 58
  soup, Crockpot, 185
  topping, tropical, 196
Fruity coffee cake, 34
Fudge, Mamie Eisenhower, 262

Garden salad, 163
Garlic beans, 166
Garlic bread, 84
German potato salad, 12
Ghosts and goblins activities, 67
Gingerbread cookies, 86
Goulash, 61
Grandma and grandpa's visit, 268
Granny's mud pie, 247
Gravy, low-fat, low-salt, 93
Green Bay Potatoes, 202
Green beans, dilly, 225, savory, 153
Green chilies corn bread, 205
Grilled foods, for fall, 2

Half-time huddle recipes, 148
Ham slices, tropical, 271
Hamburger bean cookout, 159
Hamburger, salsa, 287
Hawaiian breakfast sandwich, 131
Heath-bit cookies, 175
Hens, Cornish, with raspberry chutney, 172
Herb potatoes, oven-baked, 149
Herbal spinach chicken lasagna, 82
Herbs, 239
Holiday decorating brunch recipes, 82
Holiday shopping, 209
Holiday wrapping supper, 217
Hollywood favorites, 100
Home of the range, 222
Hot submarine sandwiches, 182
Hot wassail, 60

Ice, strawberry, 120
Italian
  meatball hero sandwich, 151
  pasta with chicken, 30
  pork chops, 233

Jack-o-lantern lunch, 69
Jello
  loaf, raspberry, 242
  parfait, spicy, 48
  strawberry dessert, 178
Jicama salad, 150
John and Sally's wild rice stuffed peppers, 246
Jolly gelatin snowman, 83

THE QUALITY TIME FAMILY COOKBOOK

Karen and Tony's all-purpose
  BBQ sauce, 226
Kathy's lemon almond
  cookies, 127
Kay's shrimp and angel hair, 18
Kids make lunch recipes, 40
Kiwi, banana malt, 32
Kohlrabi casserole, 243

Lasagna, turkey-spinach, 214,
  zucchini, 73
Late night patio party, 224
Lavon's cabbage potato soup,
  192
Learning a new sport, 170
Lemon almond cookies, 127
Lentil carrot salad, 276
Line dancing BBQ, 201
Linguini, zucchini, 47
Links, spicy smokie, 56
Lovers' patio breakfast, 49
Lunch, best buys, 192

M.J.'s chocolate zucchini
  pound cake, 140
Macaroni salad, Marie's, 224
Maids of honor, 263
Malt, banana-kiwi, 32
Mamie Eisenhower fudge, 262
Mardi Gras salad, 62
Marie's macaroni salad, 224
Marinated muskmelon, 183
Meatball hero sandwich, 151
Meatless vegetable stew, 186
Menus
  autumn tailgate, 4
  back to school, 190
  beach, 114

best friends arrive, 282
birthday bash, 29
bottom of ninth, 158
chestnuts roasting, 81
county fair, 200
ecology experience, 240
family vacation, 232
ghosts and goblins, 68
grandma and grandpa's visit,
  269
holiday shopping, 209
Hollywood favorites, 101
home on the range, 223
learning a new sport, 171
Mother's or Father's Day, 38
New Year, 55
pizza and cards, 124
rainy day comfort, 135
romance in the air, 45
snowbound, 17
Super Sunday, 144
trash or treasure, 181
White House, 251
Mexicali chicken, 40
Microwave cheese potatoes, 139
Mint cucumber shrimp sandwiches, 42
Molded cranberry salad, 94
Mom's thumbprint jams, 87
Mother's or Father's Day, 37
Movie star fruit plate, 106
Mud pie, granny's, 247
Muffin quiches, 57
Muffins
  mini, 263
  orange oatmeal, 184
  pumpkin bran, 203
  raisin oatmeal, 24

Mushroom turkey casserole, 165
Muskmelon, marinated, 183

Nasturtium salad, 244
Nectarine pie,
  cinnamon-basil, 31
New Year's
  brunch, 61
  resolutions cake, 64
  resolutions, 54
  soup supper, 63
Night before madness suppers, 182

Oatmeal
  orange muffins, 184
  raisin muffins, 24
  raisin scones, 260
Old-fashioned Crockpot stew, 275
Old-fashioned German potato salad, 12
Omelette, western, 21
One year older sleep-in recipes, 33
Open house recipes, 56
Orange
  burst fruit dip, 107
  cheese dressing, 95
  chicken salad almondine, 103
  oatmeal muffins, 184
  Orzo, turkey, stuffed tomatoes, 148
Oscar day brunch, 102
Oval Office breakfast, 259
Oven-baked herb potatoes, 149
Overnight cinnamon French toast, 49, egg bake, 285

Pancakes
  apple bran oven, 212
  brunch-stype potato, 137
  buttermilk, 270
  pumpkin, 71
Parfait, spicy jello, 48
Parmesan potatoes, 6
Parmesan topped corn on the cob, 116
Parsley potatoes, 173
Parson's Inn
  caramel rolls, 273
  overnight egg bake, 285
  sweet rolls, 272
Pasta, Italian, with chicken, 30
Patio party vegetables, 227
Pea and cheese salad, 19
Peachy pie, 154
Peanut butter cookies, 11,
  chocolate pudding, 130
Pears, tangy, 70
Pecan-stuffed French toast, 146
Peg's asparagus-potato soup, 136
Pep rally supper recipes, 5
Pepper, banana, and cucumber salad, 174
Peppercorn salad, 13
Picante vegetables, 289
Picnic recipes, 118
Pie
  cheesecake, 22
  cinnamon-basil nectarine, 31
  mud, 247
  peachy, 154
  strawberry, 206
Pita pockets, turkey cucumber, 117

Pita, avocado-witch, 69
Pizza
  and cards, 123
  BLT, 125
  breakfast, 131
  brunch recipes, 125
  chicken fajita, 128
  crust, whole wheat, 10
  fruit, 126
  veggie, 9
Popovers, 241
Pork chops, chutney-style, 201, Italian, 233
Potato
  asparagus soup, 136
  cabbage soup, 192
  cheese, microwave, 139
  Green Bay, 202
  melts, baked, 177
  oven-baked herb, 149
  pancakes, 137
  Parmesan, 6
  parsley, 173
  riced, 92
  salad, German, 12
  soup, cheesy, 8
  twice-baked, 256
Pound cake, chocolate zucchini, 140
Pregame breakfast recipes, 7
Presidential flannel cakes, 259
Pudding, chocolate peanut butter, 130
Pumpkin bran muffins, 203, pancakes, 71

Quiches, muffin, 57

Raid the pantry, 283
Rainy day comfort, 134
Raisin
  and cabbage stew, 204
  apple compote, 72
  oatmeal muffins, 24
  oatmeal scones, 260
  wheat bread, 176
Raspberry chutney, Cornish hens with, 172
Raspberry Jello loaf, 242
Red hot cinnamon applesauce, 50
Red pepper fish, 5
Relaxing fireside recipes, 138
Resolutions, New Year's, 54
Rice and broccoli casserole, 235
Rice, wild, stuffed peppers, 246
Riced potatoes, 92
Roadside lunch, 117
Rock star brownies, 110
Rodeo Drive dinner recipes, 108
Rolled sugar cookies, 85
Rolls, whole wheat, 96
Romance in the air, 45
Rotini salad, 218

Sage dressing, 91
Salad
  banana pepper and cucumber, 174
  carrot lentil, 276
  cherry-Coke, 257
  chicken, Caesar's, 138
  cucumber, 129
  garden, 163
  jicama, 150

INDEX

Mardi Gras, 62
molded cranberry, 94
nasturtium, 244
orange chicken, almondine, 103
pea and cheese, 19
peppercorn, 13
rotini, 218
taco, 118
Salmon patties, 108
Salsa hamburger, 287
Sandwich
  carrot, 261
  chocolate, 119
  Hawaiian breakfast, 131
  hot submarine, 182
  meatball hero, 151
  shrimpy cucumber mint, 42
Sassy applesauce with dumplings, 167
Saturday grazing recipes, 115
Sauce, BBQ, 226
Sauce, celery, vegetable frittata with, 193
Savory green beans, 153
School, back to, 189
Scones, oatmeal raisin, 260
Second inning baseball dinner, 162
Sesame-soy cod, 255
Set, lunch on the, 104
Sharon's patio party vegetables, 227
Shopping list
  autumn tailgate, 14
  back to school, 197
  beach day, 121

best friends arrive, 290
birthday bash, 35
bottom of ninth, 168
chestnuts roasting, 97
county fair, 207
ecology experience, 248
family vacation, 236
ghosts and goblins, 77
grandma and grandpa's visit, 278
holiday, 219
Hollywood favorites, 111
home on the range, 229
Mother's and Father's Day, 43
New Year's, 65
pizza and cards, 132
rainy day, 141
romance in the air, 51
snowbound, 25
Super Sunday, 155
trash or treasure, 187
White House, 264
Shopping, holiday, 209
Shrimp and angel hair, 18
Shrimpy cucumber mint sandwiches, 42
Sleep-in brunch, 285
Smoothies, strawberry tofu, 245
Smores, 228
Smorgasbord recipes, 151
Snacks, 119
Snipe hunt, 228
Snow drift breakfast recipes, 21
Snowbound activities, 16
Snowman, jolly gelatin, 83

Soup
  carrot, 162
  cheesy potato, 8
  creamy cucumber, 102
  Crockpot fruit, 185
  Lavon's cabbage potato, 192
  Peg's asparagus-potato, 136
  strawberry, 41
  supper, 63
  tangy broccoli, 63
Soy-sesame cod, 255
Spicy Jello parfait, 48
Spicy smokie links, 56
Spinach-chicken lasagna, 82
Spinach-turkey lasagna, 214
Sport, learning a new, 170
Squash mountains, 234
Squash, twice-baked, 161
Star studded salmon patties, 108
State dinner, semi-formal, 255
Steaks, tomato, 109
Stew
  American Indian, 217
  cabbage and raisin, 204
  meatless vegetable, 186
  old-fashioned Crockpot, 275
Story telling supper, 275, 287
Strawberry
  ice, 120
  Jello dessert, 178
  pie, 206
  soup, 41
  tofu smoothies, 245
Stroganoff, turkey, 283
Stuffed peppers, wild rice, 246
Stuffed tomatoes with smoked turkey and orzo, 148

Submarine sandwiches, hot, 182
Sugar cookies, 85
Sugared blueberries, 39
Sunday board games, 23
Super Sunday activities, 144
Supper by the river, 246
Surprise breakfast in bed recipes, 39
Sweet rolls, Parson's Inn, 272

Table setting, White House, 252
Taco salad, 118
Tag sale day, 186
Tailgate, beginner's lunch, 9
Talk over the bargains, 214
Tangy broccoli soup, 63
Tangy chicken breasts, 23
Tangy pears, 70
Tea, brewing perfect, 254, cream, etiquette, 253
Texas-style supper, 204
Thumbprint cookies, 87
Toast, French, 146, 195
Tofu smoothies, strawberry, 245
Tomato steaks, 109
Tomatoes, stuffed with turkey and orzo, 148
Topping, tropical fruit, 196
Tortellini supreme, 115
Tossed garden salad, 163
Trash or treasure activities, 180
Trick-or-treat party, 73
Tropical fruit topping, 196
Tropical ham slices, 271
Turkey
  breast, microwaved, 90
  cucumber pita pockets, 117

INDEX

mushroom casserole, 165
orzo, stuffed tomatoes, 148
roasted, 89
spinach lasagna, 214
Stroganoff, 283
Twice-baked potatoes, 256,
squash, 161

Vegetable frittata with creamy celery sauce, 193
Vegetable stew, meatless, 186
Vegetables, patio party, 227,
picante, 289
Veggie pizza, 9
Virginia's broccoli and rice casserole, 235

Wassail, 60
Western omelette, 21
Wheat, raisin bread, 176
White House dining, 250
Whole wheat pizza crust, 10
Whole wheat rolls, 96
Wild rice stuffed peppers, 246
Winter rotini salad, 218
Winter winds dinner recipes, 18
World Series Supper, 165

Zucchini
chocolate pound cake, 140
lasagna, 73
linguini, 47

Other Books from Chronimed Publishing

366 Low-Fat Brand-Name Recipes in Minutes by M.J. Smith, M.S., R.D./L.D. Here's more than a year's worth of the fastest family favorites using the country's most popular brand-name foods—from Minute Rice® to Ore Ida®—while reducing unwanted calories, fat, salt, and cholesterol.

004247   ISBN 1-56561-050-4 $12.95 ❏

All-American Low-Fat Meals in Minutes by M.J. Smith R.D., L.D., M.A. Filled with tantalizing recipes and valuable tips, this cookbook makes great-tasting low-fat foods a snap for holidays, special occasions, or everyday. Most recipes take only minutes to prepare.

004079   ISBN 0-937721-73-5 $12.95 ❏

60 Days of Low-Fat, Low-Cost Meals in Minutes by M.J. Smith, R.D., L.D., M.A. Following the path of the best-seller *All American Low-Fat Meals in Minutes*, here are more than 150 quick and sumptuous recipes complete with the latest exchange values and nutrition facts for lowering calories, fat, salt, and cholesterol. This book contains complete menus for 60 days and recipes that use only ingredients found in virtually any grocery store—most for a total cost of less than $10.

004205   ISBN 1-56561-010-5 $12.95 ❏

Fight Fat & Win Cookbook by Elaine Moquette-Magee, M.P.H., R.D. Now you can give up fat and create great tasting foods without giving up your busy lifestyle. Born from the bestseller *Fight Fat & Win*, this practical cookbook shows you how to make more than 150 easy and tempting snacks, breakfasts, lunches, dinners, and desserts that your family will never know contain little or no fat.

004254   ISBN 1-56561-055-5 $12.95 ❏

Fight Fat and Win, Updated & Revised Edition by Elaine Moquette-Magee, R.D., M.P.H. This breakthrough book explains how to easily incorporate low-fat dietary guidelines into every modern eating experience, from fast food and common restaurants to quick meals at home, simply by making smarter choices.

004244   ISBN 1-56561-047-4 $9.95 ❏

Fast Food Facts, Revised and Expanded Edition by Marion Franz, R.D., M.S. This revised and up-to-date best-seller shows how to make smart nutrition choices at fast food restaurants—and tells what to avoid. Includes complete nutrition information of more than 1,500 menu offerings from the 37 largest fast food chains.

Standard-size edition, 004240   ISBN 1-56561-043-1 $7.95 ❏
Pocket edition, 004228   ISBN 1-56561-031-8 $4.95 ❏

Convenience Food Facts by Arlene Monk, R.D., C.D.E., with an introduction by Marion Franz, R.D., M.S. Includes complete nutrition information, tips, and exchange values on more than 1,500 popular name brand processed foods commonly found in grocery store freezers and shelves. Helps you plan easy-to-prepare, nutritious meals.

004081   ISBN 0-937721-77-8 $10.95 ❑

The Brand-Name Guide to Low-Fat and Fat-Free Foods by J. Michael Lapchick with Rosa Mo, R.D., Ed.D. For the first time in one easy-to-swallow guide is a compendium of just about every brand-name food available containing little or no fat—with complete nutrition information.

004242   ISBN 1-56561-045-8 $9.95 ❑

Muscle Pain Relief in 90 Seconds by Dale Anderson, M.D. Now you're only 90 seconds away from relieving your muscle pain—drug free! From back pain and shin splints to headaches and tennis elbow, Dr. Anderson's innovative "Fold and Hold" technique can help. Simple, safe, and painless, this method is a must for all of us with muscle aches and twinges.

004257   ISBN 1-56561-058-X $10.95 ❑

Taking the Work Out of Working Out by Charles Roy Schroeder, Ph.D. This breakthrough guide shows how to easily convert what many consider to be a chore into enjoyable, creative, and sensual experiences that you'll look forward to. Includes methods for every form of exercise—including aerobics, weight lifting, jogging, dance, and more!
•A Doubleday Health Book Club Selection

004246   ISBN 1-56561-049-0 $9.95 ❑

The Business Traveler's Guide to Good Health on the Road edited by Karl Neumann, M.D., and Maury Rosenbaum. This innovative guide shows business travelers how to make smart food choices, exercise in planes, trains, automobiles, and hotel rooms, relieve stress, and more. Plus, this guide has a listing of hotels in the U.S. and Canada with fitness facilities. All this, presented with a generous seasoning of fun and interesting facts and tidbits, makes the book a must for every business traveler's expense list.

004233   ISBN 1-56561-036-9 $12.95 ❑

The Healthy Eater's Guide to Family & Chain Restaurants by Hope S. Warshaw, M.M.Sc., R.D. Here's the only guide that tells you how to eat healthier in over 100 of America's most popular family and chain restaurants. It offers complete and up-to-date nutrition information and suggests which items to choose and avoid.

004214   ISBN 1-56561-017-2 $9.95 ❑

Fat Is Not a Four-Letter Word by Charles Roy Schroeder, Ph.D. Through interesting scientific, nutritional, and historical evidence, this controversial and insightful guide shows why millions of "overweight" people are unnecessarily knocking themselves out to look like fashion models. It offers a realistic approach to healthful dieting and exercise.

004095   ISBN 1-56561-000-8 $14.95   ❏

Exchanges for All Occasions by Marion Franz, R.D., M.S. Exchanges and meal planning suggestions for just about any occasion, sample meal plans, special tips for people with diabetes, and more.

004201   ISBN 1-56561-005-9 $12.95   ❏

Beyond Alfalfa Sprouts & Cheese: The Healthy Meatless Cookbook by Judy Gilliard and Joy Kirkpatrick, R.D., includes creative and savory meatless dishes using ingredients found in just about every grocery store. It also contains helpful cooking tips, complete nutrition information, and the latest exchange values.

004218   ISBN 1-56561-020-2 $12.95   ❏

One Year of Healthy, Hearty, & Simple One-Dish Meals by Pam Spaude and Jan Owan-McMenamin, R.D., is a collection of 365 easy-to-make healthy and tasty family favorites and unique creations that are meals in themselves. Most of the dishes take under 30 minutes to prepare.

004217   ISBN 1-56561-019-9 $12.95   ❏

Foods to Stay Vibrant, Young & Healthy by Audrey C. Wright, M.S., R.D., Sandra K. Nissenberg, M.S., R.D., and Betsy Manis, R.D. From tips on increasing bone strength to losing weight, here's everything women in midlife need to know to keep young and healthy through food. With authoritative advice from three of the country's leading registered dietitians, women over 40 can eat their way to good health and feel better than ever!

004256   ISBN 1-56561-057-1 $11.95   ❏

200 Kid-Tested Ways to Lower the Fat in Your Child's Favorite Foods by Elaine Moquette-Magee, M.P.H., R.D. For the first time ever, here's a much needed and asked for guide that gives easy, step-by-step instructions to cutting the fat in the most popular brand-name and homemade foods kids eat every day—without them even noticing.

004231   ISBN 1-56561-034-2 $12.95   ❏

Order Blank on Next Page

Chronimed Publishing
P.O. Box 59032
Minneapolis, Minnesota 55459-9686

Place a check mark next to the book(s) you would like sent. Enclosed is $ _____. (Please add $3.00 to this order to cover postage and handling. Minnesota residents add 6.5% sales tax.)

Send check or money order, no cash or C.O.D.'s. Prices and availability are subject to change without notice.

Name_____

Address_____

City _____State _____Zip_____

Allow 4 to 6 weeks for delivery.
Quantity discounts available upon request.

Or order by phone: 1-800-848-2793

612-546-1146 (Minneapolis/St. Paul metro area).
Please have your credit card number ready.